Progress

and

Regression

Rahel Jaeggi

Translated by **Robert Savage**

Harvard University Press

Cambridge, Massachusetts
London, England

2025

Printed in the United States of America

EU GPSR authorized representative:
Logos Europe
9 rue Nicolas Poussin
17000 La Rochelle, France
contact@logoseurope.eu

Cataloging-in-Publication Data available from the Library of Congress
ISBN: 978-0-674-29801-9

For Andreas and Jakob
. . . and for UUU
1931–2021

CONTENTS

PREFACE

I know it was around the mid-1960s—maybe '64, maybe '65, and
definitely by '66—I noticed the summers were getting longer each
year, and not just longer but better, too. I had the impression that
the world was getting better year by year—and this was especially
noticeable in summer. —PETER KURZECK

Does progress have seasons? —DIETMAR DATH

This book confronts an issue that informs a great deal of current
philosophical and political discussion, even if this may not always
be obvious: social progress and its opposite, regression. The situation we face today with regard to progress and regression is anything but straightforward, to put it mildly.

While signs of progress can be detected here and there, most
people nowadays are far removed from thinking that humankind is
moving "by alternating stages of calm and agitation, of good and
evil," toward its ever greater perfection, as Turgot put it in one of
the founding texts of the modern idea of progress.[1] This is true not
only of those places on our planet that are sliding into abysses of
war, violence, and chaos, falling into open exploitation and oppression, and suffering only the dark side of progress while being denied its blessings. The war in Ukraine and ongoing conflicts in
Libya, Syria, Sudan, the Middle East, and many other trouble spots
around the world, the plight of women in Afghanistan and Iran,
and the global resurgence of nationalist and authoritarian move-

ments all raise concerns that the progress of yesteryear can be undone. Drownings of refugees in the Mediterranean have come to symbolize how even minimal standards of humanity are being undermined at the borders of Europe—the same Europe that elsewhere deploys military force in the name of freedom and democracy.[2] As burning forests and melting glaciers bring home the reality of the climate catastrophe to privileged parts of the world, doubts about the achievements of the Western world's supposedly progressive way of life and economic system have arisen. Here, too, it seems that hopes for progress have been dashed. Given the many interrelated crises that threaten to swamp us, President Biden's 2023 celebration of the "story of America" as "a story of progress and resilience, of always moving forward" sounds more like wishful thinking than an accurate description of the state of the union.[3]

There is debate not just over whether progress has occurred in the past or will do so in future: the concept of progress itself is hotly contested. Some theorists bullishly register the onward march of progress in many fields of human life.[4] Others instead regard the idea of progress as outdated and dangerous, or even—in Ashis Nandy's drastic formulation—as "one of the most violent intrusions in our lexicon."[5] And while some draw on an at least implicit narrative of progress to underpin their hopes of emancipation, others insist that we must liberate ourselves from such "antiquated notions of development," particularly if we are to combat the evils of social and colonial hegemony.[6] As James Tully pithily states, "the language of progress and development is the language of oppression and domination for two-thirds of the world's people."[7]

Although the notion of progress is thus notoriously problematic today, its counterpart, the notion of regression, is gaining momentum.[8] From a liberal-democratic standpoint, the political success of strongman politicians like Donald Trump, Jair Bolsonaro, Victor Orbán, and Recep Tayyip Erdoğan represents a reversion to autocratic norms. Hateful, right-wing populist resentment directed against the pluralization and diversification of identities and life-styles may be considered regressive.[9] The fact that books are being removed from school libraries in some US states for addressing gender- and race-related themes shows just how fragile the hard-fought victories of the anti-racist and feminist movements are.[10] Similarly, Oliver Nachtwey has described the dismantling of many of the traditional European welfare states and associated rise of a new precariat as symptoms of a "regressive modernity."[11]

Yet if progress is the flipside of regression and vice versa, the idea of progress reenters the scene through the back door, so to speak. If the rising tide of attacks on lives and lifestyles stigmatized as "other" is perceived as regressive, then it makes sense to consider the exten-sion of human and civil rights to groups previously excluded by the dominant culture as progressive. If the dismantling of the welfare state in Western Europe is considered regressive, this is presumably because the rise of a comprehensive social security system after the Second World War, for all its faults, is a sign of social progress. And if populist authoritarian governments are deplored as regressive, this implies regret at the reversal of the historical gains made in en-trenching the rule of law and liberal democracy around the world, however compromised by violence such gains may have been.

An all too sweeping critique of progress could thus be an ex-ample of what Sartre called *mauvaise foi*, bad faith.[12] One adopts a stance of radical skepticism toward progress while surreptitiously and unreflectively clinging to the idea of progress. This becomes apparent at the point where certainties break down. The result is not infrequently a dubious mix of theoretical relativism and polit-ical moralism.

We need to talk about progress, then. And about regression. To what extent is it appropriate to characterize the signs of the times I have just sketched as socially *regressive*—and not just a blow to our hopes? Of what use are the categories of "progress" and "re-gression" for a critical understanding of social developments, and what risks are involved in using them?

Progress, we are used to saying, is a change for the better, meaning that regression would be a change for the worse. While in a sense this is true, it is not entirely accurate. What is crucial, and what I will be arguing in this book, is that progress refers to a form of change, or more precisely, a certain way of responding to crises and solving problems. In brief, progress is a self-enriching experiential learning process for finding solutions to problems that are systemically blocked under conditions of regression.

Progress, as I will conceptualize it throughout this study, has nothing to do with a smugly self-congratulatory Whig history of Western imperialist societies.[13] Nor is regression the paternalistic verdict on those deemed to have been left behind by Western modernity. Rather, the progress/regression binary is primarily the conceptual vehicle for critique and self-critique of the very societies that pride themselves on their supposed progressiveness.

Consequently, referring to specific achievements as progressive does not absolutize the thus achieved status quo, just as referring to socially regressive processes does not mean longing for a return to the good old days before these processes began. Quite the contrary: if everything had been good back then, there would be no regression. Put in dialectical terms, regression is already inherent in the blind spots, exclusions, contradictions, and casualties of progress. Regression is therefore not a step back from something already achieved but, with Adorno, the prevention of the possible.[14] Conversely, progress is not a great leap forward toward some preordained goal but the interminable process of emancipation. Under the banner of progress, critical theory thus defends not what has been achieved in this world but the possibility of a different world.

The approach taken in this book is conceptual and draws on the tradition of social philosophy. I will defend progress and regression as meaningful or even indispensable criteria for analysis and cri-

tique of social developments, and thus (re)sharpen crucial conceptual tools that risk losing their critical edge in the blur of much
current discourse. As we are confronted with all sorts of social
crises, conflicts, and processes of change, it behooves us to identify
emancipatory movements and the roadblocks that stand in their
way. If we are to evaluate social developments and struggles, then
the ability to make categorical distinctions between progressive social changes and regressive tendencies is crucial, albeit complicated.
This is not merely a question of definitions. Concepts carry experiential content; they harbor and express (historical) experiences and
problems that need to be deciphered and salvaged. Concepts take in
something, as the etymology suggests (from the Latin *concipere*).[15]
And insofar as they cater to the self-understanding of social actors,
they have real-world effects. They are something like a catalyst for
collective self-understanding and agency. My aim is thus to clarify
conceptual questions for the purpose of practical orientation.

The question that interests me here is therefore not whether
something like progress can be empirically ascertained today and,
if so, where. It is not my ambition to decide on an empirical basis
whether the human race, all evidence to the contrary notwithstanding, is moving toward an ever more peaceful, just, and pros-
perous existence, or whether it is instead sinking deeper and deeper
into the quicksand of injustice and violence. The choice between the
two alternatives of a Panglossian faith in progress and a pessimistic
diagnosis of decline—I am sometimes asked if I "believe" in progress—
is also irrelevant for my project. Two things should be kept separate
here: on the one hand, the belief that human history is factually
progressing, such that we can reconstruct a history of progress and
anticipate further gains; on the other, the question of whether progress (if it even exists) could be identified in the first place, such that
there are criteria for identifying social and historical changes as progressive. How can we know that we are dealing with change for the
better or worse rather than with change as such?

The decision of whether or not to hold fast to the idea of progress should not be based purely on the brute facts of world events. This idea is not discredited simply because history seems to be shifting into reverse, just as the idea of happiness is not invalidated by the crushing weight of human misery in the world. By the same token, however, progress is not just a normative idea with no connection to social reality.[16] Without the real possibility of change, whatever the barriers that stand in its way—without the genuine potential for a different or new society to emerge—there would be no point in sticking to the interpretive paradigm of progress. Progress is neither a fact nor an ideal, nor is it a more or less justified empty norm. To express what it is in a Marxist register that would itself need unpacking, progress is "the *real* movement which abolishes the present state of things."[17] In a Hegelian sense, though, "reality" is not only the totality of what is "out there" in the world; it is also what, in its contradictory and crisis-prone nature, has the potential to rise above the brute facticity of what is. In this sense, the criterion of progress accomplishes two things at once: it discloses what exists in the medium of the concept, and it goes beyond it in the medium of critique. In Adorno's words: "The concept of progress is philosophical in that it articulates the movement of society while at the same time contradicting it. Having arisen societally, the concept of progress requires critical confrontation with real society."[18]

This book was inspired by a number of motives. One is to offer a diagnosis of the various threats to our form of life, the social and political regressions we are experiencing right now and those that may lie ahead. The other motives are more philosophical and methodological in nature, although these two cannot be neatly separated. What they have in common is that they have gained new prominence in recent years, albeit in very different ways.

Philosophically, the concept of progress has been revived in recent years in the Anglo-American world and in the context of debates about moral progress.[19] Not least in response to increasing dissatisfaction with "ideal theory," the question of how those instances of moral progress that most of us can normatively agree on actually came about has sparked interest in the nature and conditions of such changes.[20] But this interest does not go far enough—all too often, it remains trapped in idealist and individualist assumptions. What is important, though, is that these debates have rehabilitated the question of social transformation processes within contemporary moral philosophy.

The discussion about progress thus touches—and this is my third guiding thread—on what was once a fundamental concern of Critical Theory: investigating the causes, driving forces, character, and underlying laws of the social transformation process, including social revolutions.[21] Whether terms like *progress* and *regression* should still belong in the conceptual toolbox of a critical theory is the subject of controversial debates within Critical Theory.[22] This is not a matter of arbitrary theoretical or strategic preferences; it concerns the foundations, methodology, and justification of Critical Theory itself. Even though this metatheoretical aspect need not interest everyone, I see my reflections on progress as intervening in the debate about the approach and specific character of a critical theory—be it the Critical Theory of the Frankfurt School or more broadly conceived critical theories in the plural.

In this book, I develop a theoretical approach that emerged from my book *Critique of Forms of Life.*[23] There, I asked how forms of life can be criticized across contexts. My answer, in a nutshell, was that forms of life succeed when they can be understood as resulting from a self-enriching experiential learning process that drives further learning. Simplifying somewhat, one could say that forms of life are good, rational, appropriate when they are not regressive but progressive—as much the product as the starting point of progressive social change. This already very cautiously alludes to a concept of progress. This vague presentiment will be fleshed out here in a way that combines the findings of my previous study with the challenges we face today.

Progress
and
Regression

INTRODUCTION

> There is no legitimate criticism of progress save that which designates the reactionary moment in the prevailing absence of freedom, and thereby inexorably excludes every misuse in the service of the status quo. —THEODOR W. ADORNO

THE CONCEPT OF progress can be defended only if it is reconstructed and reimagined in light of the criticisms directed against it. Such a redemptive critique must first grapple with the implications and political-philosophical semantics of the concept of progress, and then probe those elements of the concept that need to be redefined. This is what I set out to do in this Introduction by engaging with key dimensions of the progress narrative. I conclude with a chapter-by-chapter overview of my argument and explain how my reconstruction will proceed.

I.1 Progress(es)

In some respects, the existence of progress is undeniable. Until the discovery of penicillin in 1928 (and its production in industrial quantities from 1942), infections that are now considered harmless often proved fatal. In the Middle Ages, texts were laboriously copied out by hand; the invention of the printing press immeasurably expanded the reach of the written word. My laptop today has a computing power that an entire basement full of punch cards could not have come close to matching at the dawn of the computer age. Only a few decades ago, you had to feed coins into a public telephone if you wanted to stay connected while on the move; today, many of us struggle to *dis*connect, and my son can barely imagine a social life without smartphones. He finds it equally baffling that there was once a time when women were denied the right to vote, children could legally be beaten at school and at home, and homosexuality was a punishable offense.[1]

To assert that there has been progress here or there and in this or that field is therefore a triviality, even if progress, to quote Nestroy, sometimes "looks much greater than it really is."[2] What is not trivial is the question of why and in what way these developments are supposed to be changes *for the better*, what (or who) brings them about, and whether (and how) the various developments are interrelated. Is there progress? In one sense, the question is misleading. There are undoubtedly progresses in the plural—advances are made from time to time—but they may fall short of *comprehensive* progress, or what Peter Wagner calls a "strong concept of progress."[3] Whether the many gains made at the local or small-scale level add up to progress in this expansive sense—that is what is up for debate.

I.2 Four dimensions of the narrative of progress

Progress is a normatively charged framework, an interpretive figure that establishes a particular way of looking at social and historical processes.[4] Whenever we talk about progress, we are not talking about the empirical reality of the events themselves, stripped bare of meaning, but about our understanding of that reality, our evaluation of what we see happening, and the expectations we place on it. Progress doesn't simply exist. In grasping something *as* progress, we set historical and social events in a relation to each other that we purport to evaluate and understand. Progress is a process concept.[5] As it is both interpretive and reflective, progress is one of those concepts through which a society comes to communicate about and understand itself—not always without conflict. While there may never have been a time in world history when something was not factually changing for the better or the worse, these changes have not always been understood as progressive (or regressive).

What stands behind an understanding of social change as progressive or regressive? If we are looking for a pathway to emancipation, or at least an emergency exit from the complex crises besetting the present, then how can we use the concept of progress to understand "where we are coming from and where we are going"?[6] Drawing on Reinhart Koselleck's groundbreaking study of the history of the concepts of progress and decline, I will broadly outline four characteristic features of the narrative of progress—four distillations of its problems and possibilities that will guide my attempt to reconstruct the concept.[7] They are the *unbreakable chain* of progress, its *irresistibility*, progress as a *developmental process*, and progress as a *loss-free enrichment* or *accumulation*.

The first of these features concerns the interconnectedness of the various dimensions of progress. As my selection of examples above indicates, very different developments can be considered progressive: medical and scientific feats, technological inventions, social innovations, changes in moral beliefs, and political reforms and revolutions. To understand the force of the concept and the euphoria it was capable of unleashing, to the point that it became the watchword of an entire era in eighteenth-century Europe, we need to realize that the concept of progress bundled all these distinct changes into a single, all-encompassing dynamic. Progress did not simply denote piecemeal improvements in isolated areas, or moral purification alone, but the betterment of living conditions across the board. The idea of a great wave of change sweeping irresistibly through all areas of life owed much of its appeal to the undeniable progress made by science and technology in gaining mastery over nature. Reinhart Koselleck vividly describes this tendency:

> The invention of the printing press; the spread of literacy and reading; the inventions of the compass, telescope, and microscope; the development of the experimental sciences; the discovery of the globe; overseas colonization and the comparison with savages; the conflict of modern art with the old; the rise of the middle classes; the development of capitalism and industry; the unleashing of natural forces through technology—all this belongs to the experiences or facts that are always conjured up and tied to the concept of progress and, more than that, to the progression toward something better.[8]

Steven Lukes also emphasizes the interplay of the various developments that shape how progress is perceived: "Growth in the economy and in scientific knowledge, both theoretical and practical, and an increase in justice, virtue, and happiness—all these were interlinked *as if by an unbreakable chain.*"[9] Marx shows he is heir to this Enlightenment-era progressivism when he reaffirms this "unbreakable chain," positing a connection between the technoscientific and moral improvement of the human race and its living conditions, between mastery of nature and social domination.[10]

The second characteristic states that progress is a process that, as described by Koselleck, unfolds with apparently impersonal and irresistible force. It imposes itself and is accepted with an air of fatalistic inevitability.[11] Progress then does not appear to be "man-made," in any simple or direct sense; rather, it presents itself as the execution of what, in Hegel's words, "is timely."[12] As a simultaneously anonymous and historical power, progress confronts the subjects it seizes as a "transpersonal subject of action."[13] The normative self-certainty of the protagonists of progress—in their view, these developments bring about a self-evident change for the better—is also bound up with this irresistible dynamic.[14]

The assumption of irresistibility leads to a third characteristic, one that is inseparably linked with classical ideas of progress: the idea of an *evolutionary logic*. According to this idea, progress is a world-historical learning process that adheres to a single evolutionary template and hence is normatively binding. Regardless of whether this template is one of gradual unfolding or maturation, progress is always imagined as a type of social change that follows a prescribed line of development or runs through a series of necessary steps. Turgot admits as much in a revealing formulation: "the human race, considered from its origin onward, appears in the eyes of the philosopher an immense whole, which itself, like every individual, has its childhood and its progress." This idea of a development of the human race from childhood to adulthood not only implies a larger nexus in which "all ages . . . are linked by a sequence of causes and effects which connects the present state of the world with all those states that have come before."[15] It also posits an oddly paternalist hierarchy of developmental stages.

A fourth consequence of this learning or developmental process is the idea that progress proceeds in linear and cumulative fashion, "without losses." Progress overcomes hidebound convention and replaces it with something better. Thus understood, this process of enrichment is free of ambivalence, just as there are no costs associated with progress.

I.3 Progress and its discontents

These four dimensions of the narrative of progress have all been fiercely criticized. Any systematic theory of progressive social change must stand up to this criticism.

The euphoric assumption of a solid link—the "unbreakable chain"—between technological, social, moral, legal, and political progress that once fired the utopian imagination has forfeited much of its plausibility. Few still believe that digitalization or gene technology will lead directly and automatically to moral or social progress—that is, to improvements in how we organize our communal life. Moreover, the link between knowledge and emancipation that seemed self-evident to Enlightenment thinkers has been shattered. While those animated by a faith in progress were once willing to integrate even the smallest forward step into an overall progressivist context, today we shy away from such a totalizing perspective. At best, we still hold out hope for moral progress, while technological progress is simultaneously relied on and feared. There are good reasons for maintaining that the discovery of penicillin, the invention of the washing machine, or the rise of the printing press did not, or at least not inherently, lead to any improvement in social or moral conditions. After all, the mere discovery of penicillin did not ensure that it benefited everyone. Walter Benjamin warned against fixating on "progress in the mastery of nature" while losing sight of "the retrogression of society." Advances in the productivity of labor threatened to obscure "the question of how its products might benefit the workers while still not being at their disposal."[16]

The seemingly unbreakable chain of progress described by Lukes is accordingly segmented into (local or sectoral) individual links. It is now common to distinguish between progress in mastering nature (that is, technoscientific advances and improvements in material conditions) and moral or political advances (that is, progress concerning social coexistence). Sticking to the examples mentioned above, we would record on one side the inventions of the washing machine and mobile phone and the discovery of penicillin, and on the other side, modern efforts to tackle discrimination and social power relations, the condemnation of violence against women and children, processes of democratization, and the expansion of social rights.

As a result, contemporary philosophical discussions have tended to focus more narrowly on the dimension of moral and political progress. And it would not be wrong to see the decisive theoretical precondition for Jürgen Habermas's project of a Critical Theory in its separation of social and economic reproduction from the normative reproduction of a society.

Just as the pact between technological and social progress has lost its persuasive force, so too has the idea it fostered that progress is inexorable and inevitable. Indeed, irresistibility in the form of unstoppable, compulsive growth has for many come to seem more a curse than a blessing. The idea of progress as a quasi-automatic historical movement, an evolutionary destiny playing out over the heads of historical actors, now strikes us as the fantasy of a bygone era. "If we have been living in a fools' paradise," John Dewey wrote as early as 1916, "in a dream of automatic uninterrupted progress, it is well to be awakened."[17] And Benjamin, in his "Theses on the Philosophy of History," blamed the corruption of social democracy and its historical failure on the working class's self-assurance that it was "moving with the current," swept along by the relentless tide of history.[18] Progress, we believe today, results from the actions of agents. It must be fought for and doesn't happen by itself. It is anything but irresistible; on the contrary, it is constantly dogged by resistance and more unlikely than likely in any given historical constellation.

Ultimately, whether the motif of progress is at all viable for critical theory today seems to stand or fall with the idea of a developmental logic à la Turgot (commonly also attributed to Hegel's philosophy of history). Any model in which a wide range of local developments are brought together, subsumed under a single evolutionary, normatively understood schema, and reduced to instances of an all-encompassing world-historical development lends itself to an untenable hierarchization of developmental stages. Where progress unfolds according to a preconceived plan, those who cannot or will not conform to its dictates are dismissed as Luddites. At its core, such a universalizing theory proclaims that they are not *different*, but merely are not yet where they should be. In world history, there are then almost inevitably "pioneers and stragglers, time differences, and backwardness."[19] There are main events, sideshows, and even places "without history."[20] There is "the West and the Rest."[21] Those who cannot keep pace with the march step set by so-called Western societies are consigned to "the waiting room of history," to borrow Dipesh Chakrabarty's suggestive image.[22] Colonial relations of violence and exploitation are thus paternalistically justified, and "underdeveloped" or "developing" nations are goaded toward their own happiness through domination and oppression. Supposedly uncivilized or backward peoples can be not only lectured but also subjugated, exploited, and even exterminated in the name of progress.[23] This makes progress one of the "most dangerous, double-edged ideas in our time."[24] It is an idea that, as Thomas McCarthy remarks, has the ideological function of reducing "the cognitive dissonance between liberal universalism and liberal imperialism."[25] The history of the violence inflicted by our social orders would then be inseparably bound up with the concept of progress, insofar as the latter offers a dubious pretext for various forms of ethnocentrism and imperialism.[26] In short, progress stands accused of being a tool of Western hegemony that has, to this day, provided ideological cover for exploitative and oppressive practices.

The paternalist elements resonating in the metaphor of humanity maturing from infancy to adulthood give us cause to be skeptical about a normative concept of progress. So too does the attempt to instrumentalize the paradigm of progress to establish a benchmark for development, and hence "a standardized list of characteristics, the sum of which define a modern society."[27] But the developmental model is equally questionable from a social-theoretical perspective— that is, as a theory of social change. As Adorno argued against the philosophy of history, developmental models tend to find meaning in what is meaningless, a stance that leads to cynicism when faced with the catastrophes of history and their victims.[28] The narrative of development can thus become an epistemic obstacle. According to its critics, it overlooks the asynchronies and messy temporalities of history. If, for example, we celebrate the abolition of slavery as a progressive milestone, we risk ignoring its continued presence and treating ongoing inequality, structural exclusion, and institutional racism as mere vestiges.[29]

The idea of unbroken and linear accumulation likewise offers limited guidance for understanding social change. What it misses is that every achievement brings with it moments of forgetting and unlearning. Solutions to problems generate new problems, and these sometimes come at a cost. A gain in skills may entail the loss of other skills, and problems can recur that were once solved but whose solutions are no longer accessible. Advances in industrial agriculture, for example, may have eliminated many problems, but they have also had unwanted side effects, ranging from soil depletion through over-cultivation to the emergence of antibiotic-resistant pathogens in animal feed. The progress in diagnostics made possible by medical imaging has undoubtedly saved many lives, yet it has also contributed to an impoverishment of the "clinical gaze," not to mention the financial burden placed on healthcare systems by the inflationary use of such techniques. And while drivers who rely on digital navigation systems can find their way anywhere in the world, many have lost the ability to read maps.

If progress at a global historical level cannot be detected so easily, does this mean that things just keep changing without ever getting better in any substantial sense? Given the shortcomings of the narrative of progress, can we even make a clear-cut distinction between progressive and regressive forms of social change? If not, we might have to adopt Michel Foucault's stance of "methodical precaution" toward the idea that "what we have is better than—or more than—in the past." We would need to embrace a "radical yet unaggressive skepticism" that forbids us from regarding our historical present as the endpoint of progress, and hence from "imposing on [it] a positivity or valorization."[30] The question remains, however, whether this is a stance we can afford to take.

I.4 What do we lose?

To be sure, the critique of progress is as old as progress itself. Its consequences have been anything but benign. As dark and violent as the real history of progress and its ideological appurtenances have been, we should never forget that the critique of progress also has a murky past, particularly in nineteenth- and early twentieth-century Europe. The well-documented romanticization of "the savage" and "the state of nature" is itself a classic strategy of othering from the playbook of colonialism.[31] In addition, a toxic brew of anti-progressivism, anti-modernism, anti-urbanism, and anti-Semitism characterized a critique of civilization that paved the way for European fascism. We see it undergoing a resurgence today in various neo-authoritarian and neofascist movements, from the "war on wokeness" to the populist ideologies that once again rail against Western decadence. So, the problem of progress is not dispensed with so easily. Based on the dimensions of the progress narrative I sketched earlier, we can see not only what renders it problematic, but also what we *lose* if we jettison any references to progress and regression, and to progressive or regressive social change.

First, as implausible as the premise of an "unbreakable chain" has become, if we fail to consider the obvious connections between the various changes in our way of life when reflecting on processes of social transformation, we remain blind to what I propose to call the materiality of forms of life. We then risk defining the conditions of social change too idealistically. Changed living conditions bring about changed social practices, which in turn give rise to new forms of coexistence and the normative organization of that coexistence. Falling child mortality rates due to technoscientific progress are clearly a factor in the increasing intimacy of family relations in the bourgeois age.[32] The printing press made possible the kind of bourgeois public sphere that formed an essential precondition for modern democracies.[33] And it seems highly unlikely that the information technology revolution, which has massively transformed both our ways of communicating and our practical living and working arrangements, would leave the social, moral, and political order untouched. Even if political-moral progress does not flow directly and with causal necessity from technoscientific progress, the converse notion that the two are totally unrelated is equally implausible. One of the aims of my project, therefore, is to wrest back a *materialist moment* in the concept of progress from its idealist, voluntarist, and normative reductions.[34]

Second, abandoning the idea of progress risks creating a deficit in social theory. This is troubling for the specific approach of Critical Theory, which relies on analytical criteria that allow us to make sense of historical and social changes, the erosion and transformation of institutions, practices, and forms of life. The blanket rejection of anything related to learning and developmental processes can easily lead to an oversimplified discussion in which the baby—the eminently important question of the logic of social change—is thrown out with the bathwater.

The faith in automatic progress interrogated by both Dewey and Benjamin lives on only as a straw man today, and trust in the impersonal logic of history has long since been replaced by the buzzword *contingency* and by a voluntarist faith in the intentions of actors. Yet while it is easy to discredit the notion of an automatic or transpersonal agent of history, it is harder to find an interpretation of what is going on that adequately accounts for the interplay of structures (the preconditions of actions) and events (the actions themselves).

The challenge facing any reconstruction of the motif of progress is thus to lay the foundations for a theory of progressive social change that grasps such change "neither as the fulfillment of a pre-ordained global destiny nor as an arbitrary decisionist fiat."[35]

Third, a philosophy of history that banishes others to the waiting room of history in the name of progress is not just patently problematic but also misleading. Yet how are we supposed to reflect critically and analytically on (our own) societies unless we develop some kind of narrative about how societies are transformed? This would be a story of crises, erosions, and subsequent revolutions and metamorphoses. It would also have to take into account the opportunities for action arising from such upheavals. For all his ambivalence toward the categories of progress and the philosophy of history, Adorno saw a need to hold on to them. If we too do not simply wish to accept the world "as it is," we need a narrative that breaks the spell of its facticity by illuminating its contradictions and crises along with the possibilities for changing it for the better. Even if holding on to a philosophy of history is problematic, relinquishing it is not a solution either.

Finally, as much as we should refrain from forcing diverse temporalities and differences into the Procrustean bed of a universalizing world history, we cannot rest content with mere localism and contextualism either, given the real interconnections and interdependencies that shape our planet. To paraphrase Marx, the world market is world history.[36] European development is not "the outcome of endogenous processes," as Gurminder K. Bhambra reminds us.[37] And, as Stuart Hall points out, "the story of European identity is often told as if it had no exterior."[38] Precisely for these reasons, mutual entanglements need to be retraced from a global-historical perspective.

If I speak here of what we lose when we drop the idea of progress, perhaps I should briefly address what in my view is *not* lost (or not to the same extent). While I have been discussing the materialist and social-theoretical deficits racked up by a critical theory in the absence of a theory of progressive and regressive social change, I have not yet mentioned the *normative deficit* that often dominates such discussions. For good reason: perhaps surprisingly, it doesn't particularly interest me. As I see it, we lose something more than a normative orientation of social critique when we abandon the progress/regression binary. Without progress as a regulative ideal or roadmap to utopia, we are not necessarily bereft of normative guidance. But we forfeit an analytical and explanatory category and hence also the specific way in which a left-Hegelian Critical Theory regards the question of normative grounding. As Yves Winter aptly puts it, the question of progress is not primarily or exclusively normative, but above all social-theoretical and social-philosophical.[39] It concerns not only the criteria for what is good or desirable; it also deals with how a society functions and how the conditions for changing it should be understood. This very important aspect is often overlooked in the heat of debate. Whereas contextualist, relativist, or deontological positions thus frequently mirror each other in their rejection of an idea of progress rooted in a philosophy of history, I am concerned precisely with salvaging the moment in which analysis and critique intertwine.

It is therefore not just any idea of progress that will and must be reconstructed here, but the idea of progress that developed in the wake of Hegel and Marx and was taken up by Critical Theory (for all its ambivalence). This touches on not only the question of whether things can or will get better, but above all the question of which criteria are available for determining this.

1.5 Back to progress?

In theory, as in life, wishful thinking is not enough. Can the dilemma confronting us here be resolved? How can we develop an understanding of progressive social change that takes into account the critique of progress while still taking up the challenge of re-thinking the concept in the light of social theory? The first step is to reframe the question of progress: the path to be taken is not one "back to progress" after its proclaimed end, but rather a path back to the matter that has preoccupied Critical Theory (with a capital C and T) from the beginning, and which any critical theory (in lower-case) cannot easily avoid: the question of the conditions for imple-menting progressive or regressive social change.

So, how are social change and social progress to be conceived? How do they come about, and what stands in their way? How do social and moral progress and social change relate to each other? And by what right can they be said to change things for the better? This book is my attempt to answer these questions. It argues that moral progress can be understood only in the context of a broader dynamic of social change, against the backdrop of normative and non-normative practices. Social change, in turn, arises as a reac-tion to crises and contradictions—that is, to mounting pressure from an unresolved problem. Whether this amounts to a mere shifting of deck chairs on the *Titanic* or to actual progress, in the sense of a change for the better, can only be recognized by the na-ture of this transformative dynamic itself—and occasionally only *ex negativo*, through the diagnosis of regressive phenomena. What emerges is a non-teleological, pragmatist-materialist, pluralist con-cept of progress.

I hope to solve the dilemma of progress through two main shifts in direction. *On the one hand*, I (re)define the *site of progress*. From the perspective proposed here, wherever we experience progress, entire forms of life are in flux. The intricate web of practices that are in play here are interconnected, albeit sometimes only loosely and in the form of elective affinities; they influence each other and are made possible by the same overarching developments. But if moral and political progress is embedded in changes in our ethical relations (in the Hegelian sense), and if "interventions in institutionalized social processes, the dismantling of old customs and formation of new social practices"[40] are part of a larger package that includes technoscientific and economic changes, then progress can once again be grasped as the complex, reciprocal interaction of variously connected ensembles of practices. Even if these elements do not form an unbreakable chain, we can still identify fragile yet effective linkages.

On the other hand, my conception of progress is *processual* rather than substantive. Progress in this sense does not consist in arriving at a specific predetermined state or in realizing a specific pre-determinable good. Progress is instead a mode, a way in which social change occurs—or fails to occur, in the event of regression. As I stated in the preface, progress is a self-enriching experiential learning process for finding solutions to problems that are subject to systemic blockages under conditions of regression. Importantly, the dynamic of a given development can itself tell us something about the progressiveness (or not) of the development in question. My pragmatist, crisis-oriented model of progress thus aims at a theory of social change that steers a course between teleology and contingency. This theory is sustained by the idea of a logic of history that, although fractured,[41] allows the rise and fall of institutions and social living conditions to be determined in hindsight at least.

My understanding of progress as a (dialectically) self-enriching, problem-solving process thus has two consequences for the dilemma being discussed here.[42] First, an experiential learning and problem-solving process of the type I have described is not a teleological developmental process; it does not reflect the unfurling of some innate potential, nor does it trace a trajectory toward an established goal. Instead, it lurches from one problem (in normal circumstances) or crisis (in times of accelerated change) to the next, with nothing decided in advance and no preordained end in sight.[43]

Second, because the characterization of specific social transformation processes as progressive or regressive bears no substantive relation to any particular content or evolutionary stage—but only to the mode in which change is enacted—my concept of progress as a self-enriching, problem-solving process enables us to think of a *multiplicity* of developmental learning processes. Such a theory of crisis-driven social change as an experiential learning process breaks with a Eurocentric-paternalist narrative of development. To be sure, it still implies a normative direction: things will change not only within a given sequence of transformative processes, but also for the *better* (or the worse, if society regresses). This does not imply, however, that we are dealing with a single, all-encompassing world-historical process with pioneers and stragglers, vanguard parties and left-behinds. In short, the fact that we can *diachronically* diagnose progressive or regressive processes in terms of such a problem-solving dynamic (for example, modern Europe's regression into fascism) does not automatically mean that these would be *synchronically* comparable. Progress is thereby pluralized. Nonetheless, the diagnosis of progress does not remain bound to a local context, since criteria for the quality of this development that transcend context can still be applied.

There is no "waiting room of history" in this model. Developmental or transformational dynamics can operate completely differently in different societies and lead in different directions. But they can also go awry, stall, or be blocked, as can be seen in the impasses faced by so-called progressive Western societies in their relationship with nature. It is up to a critical theory of progress and regression to identify the systemic blockages leading to such an acute failure to learn.

There is little scope here for a triumphalist Whig history. After all, if progress is a learning process, why should "Western" societies, which have clearly reached an impasse with their way of life and economic system, count as progressive? There is no need to romanticize the practical-ecological knowledge of indigenous societies to diagnose systemic learning blocks and point out the discrepancy between the realms of possibility and reality—between what we know (or ought to know) and what we do (or fail to do) with that knowledge. There is thus nothing inherently imperialist or colonialist about the idea of an experiential learning process. Conversely, the claim that non-Western societies and forms of life, suspended as it were in ruminative stasis, do not undergo such processes, indeed that the very notion of learning and development betrays a Western bias, can itself be easily unmasked as a figment of the orientalist imagination.[44]

The critique of progress, as I understand it, for obvious reasons takes its cue from the regressive tendencies of the critic's own society—Germany, in my case. If it applies the criteria for an unimpeded learning process established here on a global scale, then this is because it acknowledges how no society is cut off from the multidirectional global interconnections mentioned above, which affect economic processes no less than cultural and social ones. My approach integrates the postcolonial critique of a master narrative of development by starting out from a pluralistic narrative of progress, a multitude of intertwined yet distinct developmental dynamics. At the same time, it seeks to evaluate these dynamics according to immanent criteria that transcend local contexts.

I.6 The road ahead

In Chapter 1, I refine and examine the question of progress as a change for the better. I argue that progress is a *process concept*. It denotes a development and, more importantly, the quality of this development. I identify progress as a genuinely normative concept that, far from drawing on already established norms, establishes such norms in the first place.

In Chapter 2, I develop, in response to an influential interpretation of progress as an "expanding circle,"[45] the idea that progress is not exhausted in extending the sphere of application of preexisting norms or improving their institutional implementation. Rather, it involves their qualitative transformation. This transformation does not come as a bolt from the blue. It arises from a specific conjunction of continuity and discontinuity that is typical for processes of problem-solving and dialectical development.

In Chapter 3, I ask how social change and moral progress are to be conceived. How do they come about? How do they relate to each other? If moral progress can be understood only in the context of a whole series of other practices and beliefs, then progress is *change within change*. This again raises the question of the connection between these various dynamic processes and the mutability or immutability of moral norms themselves.

Such questions are revisited in Chapter 4, where I flesh out the theory of social change that underlies my reflections. Social change, I argue, arises in reaction to crises—that is, to a *mounting pressure for change*. The result is not a teleological model of evolution toward a predetermined goal but rather the chance to reconstruct a fractured logic of development.

Chapter 5 poses the all-important question of how the change I have been describing can be understood as progress in the sense of change for the better. In dialogue with Robert Musil's novel *The Man Without Qualities*, I defend the model of progress as a process of enrichment against narrowly particularist accounts of progress. Finally, I build on the understanding of progress as a process concept postulated in Chapter 1 to claim that whether something is a change for the better or worse can only be inferred by assessing how the dynamic of change itself is configured—and perhaps only by diagnosing the regressive phenomena that *prevent* learning processes from occurring. Societies do not have goals, they solve problems. Whether they progress or regress is not determined by how close they come to some (normative) goal but by the quality of their problem-solving, which is always the quality of their problem-solving *processes*. The Hegelian idea of a dialectically self-enriching experiential learning process thus emerges as central to the entire project.

Which takes us to *regression*. We need—and this is the subject of Chapter 6—to explain the anatomy of what we regard as regressive phenomena. Regression is not the same as retrogression, a simple falling behind achieved standards. It is a particular kind of motivated and consequential unlearning: an inappropriate and inadequate form of crisis management. The question of emancipation then becomes the vanishing point for understanding both progress and regression.

1

WHAT IS PROGRESS?

> For a theoretical account of the category of progress it is necessary to scrutinize the category so closely that it loses its semblance of obviousness, both in its positive and its negative usage.
> —THEODOR W. ADORNO

I N THIS CHAPTER, I will clarify the concept of progress with reference to contemporary debates on moral progress and make two initial arguments. The first is that progress is a *sui generis,* normative concept. Even though we associate it with change for the better, progress does not depend on a presupposed, pre-given understanding of what is right or good. On the contrary, the concept itself contributes to determining what is good or better. My second argument is that progress is a process concept. It denotes the particular quality of a development, a process of experiential learning, and thus a specific way in which social transformations take place.

1.1 What is moral progress?

How has it come about that the institution of slavery—at least as a public and legally sanctioned institution—has collapsed in most, if not all, countries of the world?[1] Or that, despite all the difficulties of enforcement, spousal rape has now been criminalized in many parts of the world, after centuries of husbands having enjoyed legally enforceable rights to possess their wives' bodies with or without the women's consent?[2] And how can it be explained that corporal punishment for children, which until fairly recently was regarded as an unobjectionable and even salutary disciplinary measure ("spare the rod and spoil the child"), is now frowned upon and has itself become a punishable offense?

In recent years, changes of this kind have increasingly been thematized in philosophy under the heading of "moral progress."[3] Despite growing reservations both inside and outside philosophy about the idea of a general or *global* social progress, there seems to be widespread agreement about such specific—*local* or *sectoral*—instances of limited change. Few philosophers would dispute that the developments just outlined are positive. And for all their skepticism, they also tend to view developments that challenge or even repeal these landmark achievements as a kind of relapse. One is tempted to say, with Adorno, "What at this time should be understood by the term 'progress' one knows vaguely, but precisely."[4]

Progress as change for the better?

But what are we actually asking about when we ask about moral progress? A first response might be that moral progress is a positively viewed change in the values generally applied when considering and assessing morally relevant questions of coexistence, along with a corresponding change in the design of institutions and social practices that regulate coexistence. The latter aspect—the localization of moral progress in social practices, its rootedness in the practical-institutional life of a society—is far from trivial. It links directly to the argument that moral change must have practical consequences and be anchored in institutions, not be confined to shifts in individual attitudes, for it to count as progress.

How widely accepted and how binding the changes in question must be, and which institutions they must be anchored in, will in reality always be a matter of degree. While it is only natural to see legal codification as a prime indicator of progress, I am also concerned with the subcutaneous domain of social practices and forms of life, with changes in microstructures—in mores, customs, discourses, and behavioral norms—that sometimes slip under the radar.[5] Such change is viewed as progressive only if it is not just any change but a *change for the better*, meaning that conditions not only differ but improve.

One can already see the danger here: whether something is deemed progressive, regressive, or neither will depend on how the change in question is assessed. Not everyone involved will see a given development as progress, particularly at the onset of transformational processes, when most innovations are fiercely contested. Some changes are ambivalent in more than superficial ways. Needless to say, the same change that amounted to progress for slaves caused losses of power and privilege for those who held them. Recent debates in Germany about spousal rape and the right to a nonviolent upbringing show how controversial the topic of family violence still is, with those defending the inviolability of the private sphere polemicizing—sometimes quite violently—against supposed crusades to bring the courtroom into the bedroom.[6]

As all this goes to show, the concept of progress has an evaluative component. "Progress" is a normative concept, not just a descriptive one. It is not enough simply to ascertain a change, such as noting that, in the 1960s, many classrooms in Germany were equipped with canes for beating unruly students, whereas this would be unthinkable today. If we regard this change as progressive, we also applaud it; we assess it as good, appropriate, or beneficial. We condemn the cruelty of hitting children and affirm the value of a nonviolent education. This evaluative, normative aspect prompted Georg Henrik von Wright to divide the discourse on moral progress into two independent components: "Progress is change for the better; regress change for the worse. The definitions split the concepts in two components: the notion of change and the notion of goodness."[7] Von Wright thus separates the descriptive aspect, which describes the change in value-free terms, from an ethical-evaluative aspect, which draws on the idea of goodness to assess this change as a change for the better. Gereon Wolters analytically dissects the concept of progress in a similar way: "Phenomena are never progressive as such, but only with respect to at least one feature that seems 'positive,' 'desirable,' or 'better' to somebody for some reason. 'Progress' means that this feature or these features, respectively, increase quantitatively or qualitatively."[8]

Such an analytical distinction between two dimensions of progress perhaps makes sense, and it is certainly not wrong to point out that progress is a normative concept. Yet it would be problematic to conclude that these two aspects—the descriptive and the normative—can be neatly separated in practice or understood in isolation from each other. On the contrary, a specific characteristic of the concept of progress seems to be that the two moments are inextricably intertwined. Although it is thus correct that a diagnosis of progress rests on an interpretation of events *as* progress, and that such an interpretation is always already governed or informed by norms, this does not mean that a descriptive moment (a supposedly norm-free description of change as mere change) can be detached from the ethical-evaluative moment (an assessment of this change as a change for the better). In my view, such a separation or scission misses the point of the concept of progress and deprives it of its specific content. This obviously holds true for its political and historical semantics, as sketched in the Introduction. After all, the idea of a transformational dynamic that sweeps everything along in its path, gaining normative traction through this very irresistibility, is what first explains the importance of the idea of progress for the normative self-understanding of an entire era. But the systematic content and systematic potential of the concept of progress, as they will be elaborated on in this book, would also be attenuated if the concept were split between change and goodness.

Progress, I would argue, belongs in the category of "thick concepts," in which description and evaluation enter into an indissoluble union.[9] In this sense, "progress" or "progressive" is a descriptive evaluation or evaluative description in which one side would be empty without the other. Progress has this in common with concepts like alienation, exploitation, cruelty, or kitsch—all of them are thick (ethical) concepts that can be claimed to constitute the texture of an always already normatively structured, evaluatively colored social world.[10]

Non-derivative nature of progress

This view takes us straight to the previously mentioned problem of the normative autonomy of the concept of progress. The separation of the two dimensions, change and goodness, amounts to a prioritization of the normative aspect, to what might be called a primacy of the good over progress. Let us assume that we want to separate the two components, as von Wright suggests and as attempts to understand progress deontologically presuppose.[11] If we are to speak at all meaningfully about progress—and also sort out the better from the worse—we would first need to know what is the good that the change aims to bring about. Goodness would be the desired state, how things *ought* to be, with which the current state, how things *are*, can be compared, allowing a particular movement to be recognized as progressive. This implies that goodness can be defined independently of progress or that it is predetermined: when we talk about progress, we must already know what the good is. In this sense, determining the good would take precedence over determining progressive change. Progress would be derivative in relation to the normative position. Progress is then "not a normative concept in its own right," as Rainer Forst logically concludes.[12]

Intuitively, this sounds plausible enough. After all, how could we know whether a change is progressive without previously having identified a desired outcome to give direction to that change? What such an approach misses becomes apparent, however, when we return to the examples outlined above. If we treat progress as a normatively derivative concept, then the assertion that nonviolent education is progressive merges seamlessly with the claim that this achieved state is (morally) good or correct. Conversely—and here it is perhaps easier to see what is lacking—contending that fascism or contemporary authoritarianism is regressive would equate to calling it morally wrong or bad. What is lost in this diagnosis is the normative and descriptive-analytical wealth of the concept of progress and its specific interpretive power. Instead of being understood dynamically, as the specific form taken by a transformation toward the good, progress would be reduced to a static normative question. The kinetic element, the temporal character of the concept, would then have no intrinsic normative significance. In the end, the concept of progress would be practically redundant in relation to the concept of goodness, making it superfluous to our normative vocabulary. The statement "x is progressive" would add no relevant information to the statement "It is good and right that x."

While progress is thus not a normative concept with its own validity within a deontological framework, the approach I am taking here, inspired by the philosophy of history, confers on it a normatively founding character. Progress is a normative *sui generis* concept in its own right, an ethically thick concept.

The first step in defending progress as such a normative *sui generis* concept is to abandon the idea that progress needs a clearly defined goal in order for it to be considered such.

1.2 The priority of progress before the good

A persistent view of progress suggests that it depends on a prior determination of its goal. Progress—yes, please! But in relation to what? And to what end? To be sure, this view is not uncontested.

The American philosopher Philip Kitcher claims that we should understand progress less as moving *toward* (a goal) than as moving *away from* (a problem).

Progress without end

I can only work out whether I am following the right path on a hike or whether I've gotten lost if I know where I am heading. Either I am making progress as I climb the mountain or I am not. On my way from base camp to summit, S1, S2, and S3 are the stages on my journey, and I can measure my progress by my decreasing distance to the destination. From this perspective, my progress is compromised if I give up and turn back or take a detour after veering off-track.

This is how some people imagine progress. And of course, there are cases in which this assumption of an end-point is immediately plausible and unproblematic: I can obviously set myself goals in relation to which I define progress. If my aim is to reach the summit, then with every step I take I am progressing toward that objective. Under the heading "progress," my running app tells me how many miles I have jogged toward my (or the app's?) weekly target. Yet even this initial plausibility is deceptive. If I were suddenly beamed up to the summit or transported there by helicopter, I would have arrived without making any progress.

When we turn to technoscientific progress, it becomes even clearer that a conception oriented on hiking, mountain climbing, and motivation apps will be misleading. The inventor of the first punch card system did not already have the ideal of a PC or modern mainframe computer in mind, nor could the inventor of the telephone have anticipated the smartphone. Although the invention of the wheel undeniably represents an indispensable first step toward the Formula One car, it was not guided by the preassigned goal of modern motor racing. The path from gnawing on raw meat to fine dining, or from the cave to the skyscraper, was also taken without any preconceived end in view.

These are better understood as (progressive) problem-solving processes in which one development gives rise to the next in response to difficulties in the here and now. Because raw meat was tough and hard to digest, people in some cultures started roasting or marinating it. They gradually refined their cooking techniques but also adapted them to changing circumstances. Clean drinking water was scarce in the European Middle Ages, hence the switch to brewing beer.[13] Real estate was in short supply in Manhattan, but the bedrock was stable, so skyscrapers began to be built on it. Vast quantities of data had to be processed to solve certain problems, especially in military technology. Efforts were therefore made to condense or expand storage capacity and improve processors without knowing where it would end. Technoscientific process thus moves from problem to problem, driven by situations where there is a wish or need to do something better, where the opportunity to do so arises, and where someone lights upon an idea for solving the problem that proves productive and feasible. It is for this reason that progress—to come back to Philip Kitcher's useful distinction—is not progress *toward* but progress *from*.[14]

I would argue that social progress is no different. It likewise results from solutions being found to emergent problems, which in turn make way for new problems and, if all goes well, new solutions. Here, too, the final destination is not known from the outset. Progress does not steer toward a preassigned goal but is driven ever onward by problems; it charts a path from the bad to the better, without the latter being determined in advance and without the process ever arriving at a foreseeable conclusion. In the words of Spanish poet Antonio Machado, "The path is made by walking."[15]

Here, the pragmatist-inspired understanding of progress as progress *from*, far from downgrading the idea of progress to a merely pragmatic onward march through history, corresponds to the negativism of Critical Theory and to what, following Hegel, we could term a dialectical understanding of experiential processes. Against the common (mis)reading of Hegel—the "lazy reading," as Terry Pinkard calls it—the dialectical process of experience does not describe a quasi-somnambulistic trajectory toward a preassigned goal.[16] For Fred Neuhouser, Hegel's argument in *The Phenomenology of Spirit* "does not begin from a fully determinate conception of what it is for a subject to be free and then, holding that idea fixed, deduce the conditions that must be met if free subjectivity is to be possible." On the contrary, "a complete conception . . . emerges only at the end," precisely to the extent that it is realized.[17]

In an important sense, freedom does not exist for Hegel until it articulates itself by encountering and surmounting the impediments to its realization. Understood in this way, the process of a change for the better involves more than merely passing from A to B, and more than clearing aside the obstacles cluttering the path to a preconceived goal. For Hegel, history is not, as Dewey falsely maintained, the "gradual making explicit and outward" of an absolute goal that has been "wrapped up" since the beginning; rather, the goal itself develops in such a process.[18]

The primacy of progress

If progress is problem-driven rather than goal-dependent, then there is also no independent good that grounds it and thus turns change into progress. But this independent good is also no longer needed, it seems. The relationship of the good to progress can almost be turned on its head: rather than only understanding progress by understanding what the good is, we only understand the good by understanding what progress is. Progress takes priority over the good.

Philosopher of science Larry Laudan advocated such a position in the course of debates in the 1970s about progress in the sciences, which in some ways parallel more recent debates on moral and social progress.[19] While progress was traditionally regarded as dependent on truth, or even "parasitic" on it, as Laudan states, this primacy of truth before progress can be inverted in the spirit of pragmatism:

> I am deeply troubled by the unanimity with which philosophers have made progress parasitic upon rationality. . . . It will be the assumption here that we may be able to learn something by inverting the presumed dependency of progress on rationality.[20]

Rationality in science is then what emerges as the result of scientific progress, rather than progress being defined by an increasing closeness to rationality. This entails a crucial revision of the shopworn presentation of two alternatives: on the one hand, the various forms of relativism and skepticism toward scientific progress, and on the other hand, a universalist belief in the rational justifiability of scientific progress. Progress—likewise understood by Laudan as a problem-solving progress—then becomes foundational for rationality, precisely because rationality cannot be determined in isolation from the development in which it marks a certain point. Laudan writes: "In a phrase, my proposal will be that *rationality consists in making the most progressive theory choices*, not that progress consists in accepting successively the most rational theories."[21]

But if rationality is to be measured against progress or progression, rather than progress being measured against rationality, then rationality itself has a "temporal core."[22] As Laudan writes:

> Progress is an unavoidably *temporal* concept; to speak about scientific progress necessarily involves the idea of a process occurring through time. Rationality, on the other hand, has tended to be viewed as an atemporal concept; it has been claimed that we can determine whether a statement or theory is rationally credible independently of any knowledge of its historical career.[23]

The same pragmatist-inspired inversion is proposed by Philip Kitcher in the realm of ethics: "Ethical progress is prior to ethical truth, and truth is what you get by making progressive steps."[24]

The normative index of the transformation in question is not nour-
ished by the concept of the good. Exactly the opposite is the case:
the good draws nourishment from the progressive transformation.
The good (and the possibility of determining the good) arises from
the progressive development rather than progress being determined
by its approximation to the good.

When it comes to social progress, there is a reason for this that
resembles what Laudan suspects about truth: perhaps we know more
about progress than we do about the good. This may be because—
and here my position converges with the negativism advocated by
Adorno—we know what the problems are, we are aware of the
abuses and inequities that need to be overcome, but we lack any
matching predetermined knowledge of the good: "But what the in-
human is we know very well indeed."[25] Perhaps it is both easier and
more productive to find out whether we are making headway or regressing in combating the bad than to identify an absolute good as
the end-state of all our striving. In the entrenched debate about the
determinability of the good (no less haunted by the specter of relativism than the aforementioned discussion in the philosophy of science), the shift in orientation to *process*, describable as a particular
form of progressive problem-solving, offers a way out.[26]

As a category in social philosophy (as well as, despite all the ca-
veats, the philosophy of history), "progress" would then not be one
concept among many, just as the progressive or regressive character
of social transformation processes is not one problem among many.
It has foundational significance—or more accurately, it takes the
place of a deontological as well as utilitarian normative foundation.

1.3 Progress as experiential learning process

By imputing a substantive meaning to progress, perhaps the question that gives this chapter its title, "What is progress?", is not even

correctly posed. Properly understood, we are dealing here with the possibility of progressive transformation, progressive social change, progress as a present participle. What interests me in this context is less the result, the realized good, than the possibility of identifying progressive transitions from one (social) state to another.

If what is normatively considered progress is thus a quality that cannot be fully grasped by evaluating a given outcome, then the process itself is what matters. Any given experiential or learning process can be interpreted from the perspective of the idea of progress and deemed appropriate or inappropriate, good or bad—or, indeed, progressive or regressive. Even in those uncomplicated cases where an ascertainable goal is at stake, there is more to progress than reaching that goal, as noted above. What we call progress encompasses not merely an effect but the pathway to that effect.

Learning

Progress is therefore associated with the idea of learning, development, or experience. Imagine if I woke up one morning and could suddenly fly. Even if I had always longed to take to the sky, it would make no sense to say that I had made overnight progress in my flying abilities. I could hardly have learned to fly so quickly. Such abrupt, unexpected changes are unlikely in relation to both individual abilities and social transformations. This example also illustrates what is meant by the claim that progress or progressiveness cannot be fully grasped by evaluating a given outcome. Progress has a temporal dimension; as a kinetic concept, it "necessarily involves the idea of a process occurring through time."[27] This is not "homogeneous, empty time."[28] It is not simply a span to be traversed from an earlier to a later point in time. It is a time in which something happens, when the elements of the process enter a state of flux, bond with each other, and emerge from each other. In the best-case scenario, this is experienced as an enrichment (or enriched into an experience). When we learn or experience something in an emphatic sense, we are not the same afterward as we were before. For an individual, "learning" means acquiring specific skills that build on each other and take practice.[29] And "having an experience" involves being affected by something that triggers a process of change in which that experience is appropriated, made one's own.[30] From this point of view, all true learning is experiential. With due caution, much the same could be said of social, collective, and historical processes.

We can see again the difference from the normativist positions I criticized above.[31] That the successful fight against chattel slavery in the United States was a victory for progress means something other than that the abolition of slavery was good or morally right. Designating it as such refers not to a state but to a progressive or emancipatory *development*. (One indication of this is that the struggle could be continued and indeed had to be continued in follow-up emancipatory campaigns, from the civil rights movement to the Black Lives Matter movement of our own time.) And vice versa: analyzing fascism or related contemporary phenomena as regressive does not just mean that they are morally wrong but that they represent a fatally inadequate development, a failure to cope with crises, a systematic blockage to experience and learning. Accordingly, it is at least conceivable that something desirable could eventuate in social life that does not result directly from a progressive development. From a purely normative perspective, the abolition of slavery, the end of institutionally legitimated violence in marriage, or the victory over fascism would still be morally right if they had fallen from the sky or been engineered by little green men from outer space. The achieved state would be welcome even if it were an unintended side effect of a change aimed at entirely different goals. The change in question would not, however, result from a progressive social development. There are thus not only changes that are not for the better but also changes for the better that are not progressive.[32]

The form of change

Progress is therefore not just any change—this could equally be a merely causal sequence of events—nor is it simply a normatively neutral conveyor belt to the good. Rather, progress is a particular kind of learning or experiential process. Progressiveness is its specific quality. This means that normative standards for change cannot be established without reference to the form taken by that change. It goes without saying that not every kind of change is progressive. What does bear saying, though, is that the progressiveness of change is not measured against its goal—prosperity or social justice, for example—but against its own quality. A certain kind of change is then deemed progressive, one that can be described as a self-enriching experiential learning process. By contrast, change will count as regressive when it is characterized by a failure to learn and a reactive insulation against experience.[33] In short, if progress marks not only the direction of movement but also its quality, then the possibility emerges of an immanent evaluation of the progressive movement that does not rely on some preestablished standard. Progress then not only has a normative content of its own, much like learning or what Adorno calls "unreduced experience."[34] This normative understanding of progress also involves a *different kind* of normativity than that invoked by those who see progress as derivative of a predetermined good and therefore have to apply external criteria to it. There is thus more to the shift I am proposing here than a reversal of priorities. Through that reversal, our understanding of norms themselves and the way they operate and can be justified also changes.

Genesis and validity

This emphasis on the dynamic of the process, the "progressive steps" themselves, should not be oversimplified. The claim that social transformation processes have a normative character because

they can be progressive or regressive in a normatively informed
sense has as its corollary that our normative concepts are *not static*
but historically constituted. From the fact that norms, along with
the nature of our coexistence, have changed throughout human history, we can deduce more than an interesting but ultimately tan-
gential observation about the genesis, origin, and formation of
these norms, more than a contextualization that leaves their validity intact. Norms are not timelessly valid, a point I will expand
on in Chapter 3. But instead of drawing relativist conclusions from
their historicity, I am defending the thesis that the type of historical
development itself generates its own normative validity. Expressed
in a philosophical shorthand that will require further elaboration,
genesis and *validity* are inseparable here. Norms are valid because
and insofar as they are the result of a particular development.

A parallel from democratic theory may be helpful here.[35] According to one influential school of thought, particular decisions
are valid in a democracy because they emerge from particular democratic procedures. Here, too, genesis and validity are conflated.
Applied to progress, this means that the various states we identify
as progressive can claim normative validity because they result
from a progressive development. And just as we can provide criteria with respect to democracy for the conditions under which the
procedure is democratic and the results are accordingly valid, so
too can we provide criteria with respect to change for when this is
progressive and the results are likewise valid. In the former case,
such criteria might include deliberative public engagement, adherence to the rule of law, procedural integrity, and inclusiveness; in
the latter, I would nominate openness to experience (or an absence
of roadblocks to experiential learning) and a dynamic of enrichment. I will come back to these criteria in Chapter 5. For now, I
want to underscore that moving from an understanding of progress
which can fall back on preexisting external norms to an understanding of progress as a mode of change does not leave us bereft of

criteria. The criteria are simply acquired by a different route. They are slimmed down and formalized, and they repose less on a normative foundation than on a conceptual truth: the idea that human beings, by virtue of their freedom, can make their own history in the mode of individual and collective self-determination, despite all the obstacles that stand in their way. As so often, the point here lies precisely in shifting the problem. The thesis of the primacy of progress over reason or the good, as introduced above with help from Laudan and Kitcher, must then be fleshed out. At least in relation to social progress, more needs to be said about what the process of change must be like if it is to count as progressive, and about the forces arrayed against it.

I proceeded from the assumption that progress is change for the better. In itself, however, this is not enough. In searching for a conception that was neither teleological nor deontological, where progress itself is ascribed normative significance, it became clear that progress is not dependent on a predetermined goal. Defined as a problem-solving process, it can be understood as progress *from*. The burden of proof now lies in describing this problem-solving process in a way that qualifies the nature of the problem-solving in question, especially as it applies in the realm of the social. The core of my proposal will be to describe this as a *dialectical process of enrichment*. This idea will gradually be addressed over the course of the next chapters.

2

REFORM OR REVOLUTION

Continuity or Discontinuity of Progress

> It will become evident that it is not a question of drawing a great
> mental dividing line between past and future, but of *realizing* the
> thoughts of the past. Lastly, it will become evident that humanity is
> not beginning a *new* work but consciously bringing its old work to
> an end. —KARL MARX

PROGRESS IS A process, a movement in historical time. But what
kind of movement? What should we make of the development
that saw social practices that for centuries had been practiced
without compunction and regarded as morally unproblematic—
slavery, child-beating, discrimination against homosexuality, to
name but a few—become stigmatized and prohibited in many societies, at least at an institutional level? How did the shift occur? Do
these changes result from a far-reaching "moral revolution" that
spawned something new?[1] Or do they reflect the gradual realization of preexisting normative potentials?

In this chapter, I will address these questions by engaging with
two prominent interpretive models, both of which emphasize the
moment of continuity. One states that moral or social progress represents an *expansion* in the scope of normatively relevant considerations, the other understands progress as a *deepening* in the institutional implementation of preexisting ideals. I will begin by criticizing
the "expanding circle" thesis on three fronts: it tends to overlook
the agency of actors and the contentiousness of processes of social

change; it fails to recognize that principles themselves change over the course of their expansion; and it cannot explain the emergence of new normative principles, the very principles whose expansion it greets as a sign of moral progress (2.1). I will then argue that while the "institutional deepening" thesis, in contrast to the expansion thesis, offers solutions to the first two problems, it too cannot explain how new normative principles are formed (2.2). Yet this need not be the case, at least not if progress is understood as a problem-oriented, self-enriching experiential process. In the last section, I will therefore contend that moral or social progress, in the sense of an improvement in the principles and institutions regulating human coexistence, can neither realize something entirely new nor be limited to applying previously known principles.[2] In the spirit of Hegel, we are dealing here with continuity in discontinuity or discontinuity in continuity. This also goes some way to resolving the notorious (albeit somewhat old-fashioned) alternative between reform and revolution (2.3).[3]

2.1 Expanding the circle

How does progress come about? "The expanding circle," as Peter Singer calls it, is perhaps the most influential philosophical theory about the course of moral or social progress.[4] In various forms, it asserts that it is not normative principles themselves that change but rather the set of those to whom moral considerations and concerns apply. Michael Walzer spells out this position very clearly: "Insofar as we can recognize moral progress, it has less to do with the discovery or invention of new principles than with the inclusion under the old principles of previously excluded men and women."[5] Where we observe moral progress, previously excluded groups such as foreigners, slaves, children, women, and (more controversially) non-human animals are gradually and consequentially raised to the status of moral fellowship. The morally relevant "we," the circle of those deemed worthy of a certain kind of treatment, expands to become more inclusive. Put bluntly, what changes is *who counts*: "Before the ethical change, black men and women did not count as full people; after it, they did, and old proscriptions now applied to them too."[6]

According to this view, what does not change is what it means to count, and the kind of treatment we owe those who do. The relevant moral principles are already recognized "old proscriptions" that are now (merely) extended to new- and latecomers. Moral progress occurs by rectifying epistemic errors, as it were.[7] We already have the right norms for treating entities which deserve our moral consideration, we were just mistaken about which entities should be included. For various reasons, we failed to register that members of previously discriminated groups, whom we measured by different criteria than those that applied to us, are in fact just like us and belong to the same moral community. We failed to understand that excluding them was inconsistent with the application of our moral principles. Moral progress is accordingly furthered, for example, by drawing attention to such inconsistencies and contradictions. It is often prepared and triggered by the empathetic realization that the excluded and outcast act and feel the same way we do.[8] Moral progress is thus a question of application.

Such progress would indeed not be an innovation in any real sense. The expanding circle remains framed by already-known norms and does not develop any new ones. If someone is "like us," we owe them respect and certain rights; we should uphold their dignity, not subject them to acts of cruelty, and treat them as free and equal subjects. In this conception, moral progress changes *whom* we owe something to, but it does not change *what* we owe them. Whatever it may be that moral progress brings about, it is not a radical break with what came before.

Plausibility of the expansion theory

This conception has a lot going for it. The description of moral progress as a process of inclusion is in many ways confirmed by historical
experience. Moves to dismantle discriminatory measures are often
preceded by the realization that the person or group previously stigmatized as repulsive and alien actually resembles us in key respects.
There is a reason why arguments like "They are no different from
you and me!" are used to urge an end to discrimination. The effectiveness of such argumentative strategies can be seen, for example, in
the successful rebranding of "gay marriage" (or "same-sex marriage") as "marriage equality" in countries such as the US and Aus-
tralia. And animal rights activists consistently highlight dimensions
shared by human and non-human animals with the aim of bringing
the latter into the sphere of moral consideration. In Rorty's words,
morally improving the world mainly involves making differences
morally irrelevant.[9] This can also be seen in the reverse process that
regularly paves the way for the bestial cruelties inflicted by humans
on each other: members of the targeted group are excluded from the
relevant in-group and progressively dehumanized. *Neighbors became
Jews*, as the title of Hazel Rosenstrauch's book trenchantly puts it.[10]
Finally, regarding moral progress as an expanding circle has the undisputed advantage that the dilemma of how to justify evaluative
standards—why should these changes count as progress?—does not
arise. This position, however, also comes with serious disadvantages.

Limits of the expansion theory

If we think of moral progress as an expanding circle, it frequently
comes across, first, as a condescending gesture, an act of charity
toward those now suddenly found also to count. The authority to
decide who is admitted into this charmed circle is wielded by a supposedly homogeneous "we," or more specifically in a majoritarian

society, by those who have a say in questions of morality (and much else besides). In the process, the agency of those who themselves were never in any doubt about their personhood is ignored, as is the opposition they face in campaigning for such expansions of the circle, few of which occur without social struggle.[11] But even if the expansion is not always conceived as granted from on high, Rorty's liberal impulse to make differences irrelevant typically translates into the problematic demand that candidates for inclusion shed their differences and become much like everyone else.[12]

Second, it is doubtful whether all moral innovations actually follow the pattern described here.[13] In his book *The Ethical Project*, Philip Kitcher mentions several examples where we cannot speak of an expansion of the circle.[14] For instance, the rejection of *lex talionis*—the legal principle of payback as response in kind—could be identified as morally progressive, but it cannot be understood as merely extending the scope of moral consideration.[15] Here, it is not the case that a new group of individuals has been included in the realm of moral consideration. Instead, a different legal principle now pertains, based on a different idea of responsibility and personal identity. As Kitcher rightly points out: "No circle is expanded; one circle is replaced with another."[16]

I would go further: even cases which initially seem to support an interpretation of progress as the extension of preexisting principles often prove to be less plausible on closer inspection. When slavery is abolished, slaves are not just suddenly "human beings like us." Instead, our understanding of what it means to be a human being or person changes, along with our sense of which entities can be accorded the status of alienable objects. The same goes for the inclusion of children in the moral community. That children could be entitled to something like rights—and not subjected without appeal to the whims of paternal authority—presupposes a changed understanding of childhood, family, and familial relations. Similarly, integrating animals into the morally relevant "we," as Singer advocates, means that this "we" is now grasped as the community of all beings capable of suffering or all beings that can have interests, not (or no longer) as the community of all potentially autonomous persons or all members of the species *Homo sapiens*.[17] But this means that the circle does not just *expand*, it is also qualitatively *transformed*. The moral principles that apply to those now included in the circle are not the same "old proscriptions" from before. In order for the new members even to come into consideration, the moral principle according to which someone is considered or included has to undergo qualitative change. The principle or criterion of inclusion of a cognitivist moral philosophy, for example, is then called into question, and a moral paradigm oriented toward the human capacity for autonomy makes way for one based on the capacity for suffering shared by human and non-human animals alike. There is no continuity between these two paradigms. They are alternatives. Whereas the "expanding circle" theory thus assumes that we already have all the normative resources we need, so far as the moral principles to be applied to the ever-expanding circles are concerned, what this theory ignores is the need for innovation, for a qualitative shift in our ethical or moral principles.

There is a *third* problem that the "expanding circle" theory cannot solve: it cannot explain how new norms emerge. It cannot account for how norms arise before rippling outward and why they should command respect. As we will see, the second conception of moral progress discussed here can address the first two problems. It too falls down, however, in answering the question of how new normative principles are formed and acquire validity.

2.2 Deepening of ideals

This conception of moral progress is found in Hegelian or neo-Hegelian approaches such as Axel Honneth's. In contrast to the "expanding circle," it could be characterized as the idea of a qualitative deepening. Here, too, a certain continuity of the new with the old is posited with respect to moral-social progress; here, too, moral improvement is not owed to any radical innovation at the level of normative ideals or principles themselves. The change follows a different pattern, however. According to this conception, moral progress manifests itself as a deepened and improved interpretation and *institutional implementation* of moral principles called for by social movements, as an interpretation of their content that is not only more expansive and inclusive but above all qualitatively better and more substantial.

This model of progress can be illustrated through the example of marriage. If the bourgeois institution of marriage, as it has become ever more entrenched since the eighteenth century, rests on the idea of love, the autonomy of the parties involved, and their freely entered commitment to each other, then the institutional practice of marriage under conditions of bourgeois patriarchy does not (yet) live up to this ideal when it effectively drives women into extreme dependence and deeply asymmetrical relations of dominance. As a union between equals, marriage only comes "to itself" when women achieve real equality in matrimony with respect to decisions affecting their own lives and those of their loved ones. Much the same could be said for many other domains. The idea of a caring and respectful upbringing that is at the heart of modern parenting, for example, is better realized when children are raised in an atmosphere free from violence and coercive control. For that matter, a case could be made that the institution of free labor that underpins the bourgeois-capitalist labor market, as expressed in free and equal contracts between employers and employees, would first be realized when it no longer involved exploitation and precarity. Freedom and equality have what Jürgen Habermas calls a "normative surplus" that is only gradually redeemed as a pledge to the future.[18]

Where progress occurs, then, we move ever closer to what is intended by certain normative principles or is inherent in them, and we realize them in a more substantial or complex way in our institutions.[19] The ever-improving interpretation and institutional realization of norms initiates a qualitative, sometimes even quite radical, transformation of the practices and institutions in question, but this conception foresees no need to reinvent the ideas that underlie them.

Unlike in the expanding circle theory, however, the guiding principles do not simply remain the same. Properly understood, the idea of a deepening realization of certain foundational moral ideals, as traced by Honneth for the idea of freedom in (European) modernity, does not imply that we already have all the normative resources we need. As they are progressively realized, these ideals themselves undergo a transformation—seen, for example, in the extension of an understanding of subjective freedom initially based on natural law to the idea of social freedom.[20] Unlike in the expanding circle, we are not already in possession of the right normative principles, nor do we merely correct prior errors about who belongs in the community of those to whom they apply. With Hegel, the increasingly adequate realization of an idea involves a transformative, self-enriching process of actualization in which something is not just brought to light and understood but takes shape, assumes concrete form, and thereby changes in the course of its realization. Starting out from the old, the deepening enacts a process of transformation rather than one of rectification. The relevant ideals and norms are changed, as are the practices and institutions in which they are embedded.

The need for a qualitative change or reinterpretation of our ethical principles, for which I had advocated earlier against the expanding circle theory, would thus be met by the deepening theory, at least if we emphasize the productive element of the realization process. Realization in this sense would always encompass both elements: here something becomes real that already exists, while at the same time, something is created that did not and could not exist before its realization. Unrealized ideals are empty and indeterminate (or underdetermined). (Such realization processes can also be conceived in line with the articulation model proposed by Charles Taylor, following Herder: through its articulation, the previously formless assumes a form; this is neither a creation *ex nihilo* nor the mere bringing to light of something that might have existed prior to its articulation.)[21]

In this model, social progress is not granted "from on high," as in the rival model of expansion; Honneth quite explicitly sees it being fought for through "struggles for recognition." The contentious nature of progress is thus acknowledged, even if the role of these struggles varies in different phases of Honneth's work.[22]

Limits of the deepening model

Still, what this model cannot explain is how the historically deepened norms and institutions came about in the first place and why they can claim validity (including in the face of potentially conflicting principles) as a lodestar for change. As with the expanding circle theory, the set of norms to be realized by being deepened is initially taken for granted. Honneth, for one, clearly sees the breakthrough to modernity as progress.[23] Yet his approach does not sufficiently account for how this breakthrough took place and for the principles that impelled it. How were the relevant norms originally instantiated, and how—if at all—could the (old) normative reference points be replaced with new ones? Honneth is adamant that genuine moral revolutions, in the sense of a radical transformation of the given normative framework, are not to be expected in our current situation.[24] Moral progress would then be "reformist" in the (non-political) sense that it consists in a process of ever-deepening redemption in which the normative framework itself remains unquestioned, however radical the changes *within* this framework may turn out to be. Thus understood, Honneth's theory is not one of moral revolutions but of the moral reforms that follow on from such revolutions, and the scope of his account of moral progress is limited accordingly.

It is not as if having a theory of moral revolutions is obligatory. Nonetheless, categorically separating the instantiation of ethical or moral norms from their subsequent interpretation, implementation, and deepening realization, and thereby excluding the possibility of a radical paradigm change, strikes me as both arbitrary and implausible. My argument is that there is no need—indeed, it is not even possible—to decide in advance whether or not a (progressively emancipatory) process of social transformation moves within an established normative framework and can be confined to it. Precisely from a perspective inspired by Hegel or Marx, this is not a compelling alternative—and certainly not one that Honneth needs to posit.

2.3 Continuity in discontinuity, discontinuity in continuity

Indeed, the idea of a completely unprecedented transformation, a clean break with the past, an invention of radically new practices and principles with no connection to those it purports to supersede, may not be coherent. As Marx puts it in the epigraph to this chapter: "Humanity is not beginning a *new* work but consciously bringing its old work to an end." Even the most radical social movements legitimate themselves by claiming to realize preexisting ideas in more adequate form, put them into action, or do them justice for the first time, and they confirm this with their practical and symbolic references. Even the French Revolution was not a complete rupture that remade social life from scratch. The revolutionaries may have fired shots at clocktowers and introduced a new calendar.[25] Still, they also—even in their most revolutionary moments—drew on old customs.[26] They sought to realize ideas that were hallowed by tradition.[27] They saw themselves redeeming outstanding claims precisely by creating something new and unprecedented. In this sense, revolution is always also restitution, especially if it is to be more than a rebellion or *coup d'état*. But many examples show that the opposite holds true as well: reconstruction and realization can sometimes lead to radical innovation and transformation.

Even in cases where the interpretation of moral progress as the reinterpretation of our practices in fulfillment of a preexisting normative content is especially plausible, it is not always obvious where the border lies between institutional *adaptation to the idea* of an institution and its genuine *renewal*. If the realization of the ideal always entails a renewal of these institutions and a reinterpretation of their meaning, which in turn affects the ideals themselves, then the frame of reference does not always remain untouched by such transformation processes. In some cases, the same development can be viewed from both perspectives.

On the one hand, for example, the opening of marriage to same-sex partnerships can easily be understood as realizing the (modern) idea of marriage based on free choice and love. And even modern polyamorous relationships, in contrast to archaic or premodern polygamy, build on the romantic, individualistic exclusiveness of bourgeois monogamous marriage while simultaneously transcending it. At the same time, it could be argued that, with queer marriage, the idea of marriage and intimacy itself changes.[28] The fact that the institution that governs how "our" societies reproduce and socialize the next generation is now open to all, in principle, changes the naturalistic and exclusionary content of the institution of marriage itself. Similarly, the understanding that gender no longer has to be an inescapable destiny and that individuals now have the opportunity to determine their own genders undermines the societal notion of what gender is. In both cases, the new form undermines the old, or rather, the supposed naturalness of the old, with dramatic repercussions. Crucially, however, what changes in the described processes of progressive social change impacts the interpretive framework within which individual normative concepts operate.[29] Given the nature of the repercussions, it seems likely that not only norms concerning gender and family are put to the test here but also the conceptual framework within which certain norms are found appropriate or inappropriate. The corresponding changes can be seen from a dual perspective—in terms of deepening *and* transformation, continuity *and* discontinuity—but then the line between transformation as deepening and transformation as innovation starts to blur.

In cases of doubt, a materialist factor speaks for the novelty of the changes: marriage equality could only be recognized by courts, parliaments, and plebiscites because the idea of marriage had gradually transformed over the preceding century. This was in part because marriage assumed an altered material function that allowed it to be detached from a particular biologistic idea of reproduction, but also from a particular patriarchal model of provision or "breadwinning." Previous changes paved the way for new forms of partnership, which in turn changed existing institutions once they had become entrenched. Importantly, however, it is then at least unclear whether the new instantiations of marriage and family took on new normative significance under new historical and social conditions, rather than merely fulfilling their inherent promise or redeeming the normative surplus contained in antecedent institutions. In a process where norms are reinterpreted and ideals institutionally implemented, the relationship between the new and the given can be very complex: as ideas are put into action, new aspects of practice emerge which then need to be addressed through this very reinterpretation, deepening, and adjustment. It becomes difficult to gauge what is genuinely new and

what is a reinterpretation of the old, however radical that reinterpretation may be. And the prediction that there will be no more
moral revolutions appears to be premature, at least, in the face of
ongoing changes in material conditions (sometimes radical). New
forms build on the old, transforming and preserving them at the
same time. In short, moral progress is neither essentially reformist
nor essentially revolutionary. It should be imagined neither as producing unheralded novelty nor as merely perpetuating the old.
Even in the case of revolution, the new is not absolutely novel, and
even in the less dramatic case of incremental change, the old does
not remain what it was.

Crisis as mediation between old and new

If the social transformation processes described here proceed con-
tinuously as well as discontinuously, then this is because (as we will
see in Chapter 4) the reinterpretations of our institutions and corresponding changes do not appear from nowhere. They respond to
crises and signs of erosion in the old order: problems confronting it
from without, conflicts eroding it from within. The new arrives because the old is breaking down. It emerges at the fraying edges of a
social order that is often shot through with contradictions. Precisely
for this reason, because change is driven by crises and connected
with the old through the problems to which it responds, even a
radical shift in norms and practices does not necessarily imply discontinuity. Conversely, since the radical crises being tackled here
could always be those brought about by the old order, the link with
the old does not necessarily remain bound by the framework of
continuity.

If, as claimed, even a revolutionary, one-of-a-kind event like the
French Revolution represents both moments, that of continuity
and that of discontinuity, this is because it responds to a contradiction and turns a crisis into a conflict. The Abbé Sieyès posed

three famous questions and answers: "1. What is the Third Estate? Everything. 2. What has it been until now in the political order? Nothing. 3. What does it want to be? Something."[30] These were rhetorically skillful and practically effective because they addressed a situation of unresolved conflict, a blatant contradiction. Those who had previously been "nothing"—deprived of any say in the affairs of state and society, lacking any form of collective self-determination and any share in collective resources—were now to become "something," as fully entitled citizens. This call for the "part of those who have no part" is new to the extent that it demands something that has not existed before.[31] At the same time, revolutionaries invariably press the need for change by insisting on the restitution of legitimate claims. Even the calling of the Estates-General was already a nod to an established, albeit historically neglected institution. Its restitution, initially impelled by the financial crisis of the crown, was then driven beyond itself by the demand for voting to be conducted by headcount rather than by social order.

Yet there are other reasons why advocating the "part of those who have no part" is not a pure innovation, a demand from nowhere. Not by chance, it operates by referring to something that already exists in the social structure. Those who have no part are only lacking in social *recognition*, despite being the ones who, properly understood, constitute the nation. They are the forces that sustain the nation and generate its wealth—a fact that becomes even clearer in times of economic crisis—and they demand to be recognized in this role. They thus assert an existing reality and the realization of a *potential*. This potential—and here lies the difference between this interpretation and the notion of realizing and institutionally implementing ideas—lies in social reality, in the real forces of the "real movement" that precipitate the next virulent crisis and at the same time react to it.[32] The institutions and practices *after* a social transformation are then new and old at the same time; they both arise from a crisis of the old institutions and adapt to new conditions. That is why social transformation processes involve both continuity in discontinuity and discontinuity in continuity—the former because such changes react to looming crises and problems, the latter because such problems cannot always be solved within the existing framework. As part of a crisis-induced experiential process, the relevant social transformations—however sweeping—are connected with what came before, in that they can be understood as the solution to a problem at hand. They are (or can be) disconnected and qualitatively new, however, to the extent that these solutions cannot necessarily be drawn from the existing stock of societal resources.

This has an implication for the somewhat dated alternative of "reform or revolution?"[33] It means this: whether a particular crisis can be solved through reform (that is, normal solutions to problems operating within an established social or political order), through "non-reformist reform," or only through revolution (that is, a radical paradigm shift) will depend on the nature and severity of the social contradictions to be overcome or the crisis to be addressed.[34]

For a theory of progress, such a perspective has the additional advantage that it keeps the gap between moral-political change and other elements of societal change from widening into an unbridgeable chasm. Instead, it allows for the most varied kinds of transformative processes to be interlinked. Whatever one thinks of the likelihood of radical moral revolutions or radical innovations in our collective social existence, it would be foolish to rule out any such innovations in the future when it comes, say, to technological change. Were we to assume the same for moral progress, we would be stuck with an unvarying set of moral principles for dealing with a constantly and dramatically changing world. A further point is crucial: in a problem-solving and learning process, it is not just ideas that change. When our ideas and norms relating to marriage and family change, they do so not in isolation but as part of a whole network of practices which are influenced by these ideas and norms and which influence, suggest, or enable them in turn. Material, practical changes influence ideas, just as ideas influence practice and hence the material world. This brings us to the topic of the next chapter: how moral progress is embedded in ethical life and how ethical life is embedded in the material world.

3

IN CONTEXT

Moral Progress and Social Change

> When people speak of the ideas that revolutionize society, they merely express the fact that within the old society the elements of a new one have been created, and that the dissolution of the old ideas keeps even pace with the dissolution of the old living conditions.
>
> —KARL MARX

I N A WIDELY discussed and rightly praised article that has strongly influenced the current debate on moral progress in the United States, the American philosopher Elizabeth Anderson asks: "How do historical processes of contention over moral principles lead groups to change their moral convictions?"[1] My answer to her question will be that a change in a society's moral convictions only takes place when it is not *just* moral convictions that change. Moral change is not exclusively attributable to disputes over moral principles and claims, but also to changes in entire nexuses of practice that are themselves normatively framed and interpreted. Put differently, moral progress does not occur autonomously or arise in a vacuum; it stands in the context of a changing form of ethical life in which various dynamics interact with and influence each other. If the change we call progress can thus be situated in a complex network of interwoven practices and convictions that might be termed a social form of life, then the question of the "unbreakable chain" raised in the introduction needs to be rearticulated in the light of a theory of social practices.

In this chapter, I first develop the argument, in engagement with Marx, that moral change should not be viewed in isolation, as a purely endogenous phenomenon, but in relation to more far-reaching social changes (3.1). In the next section, I use the example of spousal rape to show how moral practices are embedded in other social practices, or in what I call the "ethical context" of a form of life. I argue that opportunities for change accordingly present themselves as disrupted relations of fit or mismatches (3.2). I develop from this an insight into the temporal core and material nature of the moral convictions in question (3.3). There follows a theoretical intermezzo (3.4) in which I briefly sketch the concept of forms of life as "ensembles of social practices" to lay the conceptual groundwork for the multiple interlinkages and mutually conditioning relationships that will be explored in the final section (3.5).

3.1 A lapse in taste? The transformation of moral progress

In Book Three of Marx's *Capital*, we find the following remarkable sentence: "From the standpoint of a higher socioeconomic formation, the private property of particular individuals in the earth will appear just as tasteless as the private property of one man in other men."[2] What particularly interests me in the sentence is a minor, seemingly trivial, yet telling detail: Marx's claim that the idea of treating human beings as private property must strike us today as "tasteless" (*abgeschmackt*). This characterization is puzzling, given that most of us (Marx included, presumably) would think that the private ownership of fellow human beings—slavery or serfdom—is not only somehow "tasteless" but utterly abhorrent.[3] Why then does Marx make this essentially aesthetic judgment, as if lamenting a mere lapse in taste in a social institution that is somehow unseemly and contemptible but also a tad ridiculous, ugly, even tawdry?[4]

The normality of moral evils

Marx was a masterful polemicist and stylist, so I suspect that this expression cannot be dismissed as a slip of the pen (or lapse in authorial taste!). The fact that owning people seems "tasteless," in our day as in Marx's, suggests an institution that has in some ways become inconceivable to us. As tasteless, the social institution of slavery is not primarily morally indefensible; rather, it has become unintelligible against what, following Hegel, I call the ethical context of our lived practices, convictions, and institutions. Treating a human being as private property—treating some*one* as some*thing*—is then not more or less reprehensible than cheating, robbing, or murdering them; to the extent that we have put slavery behind us, it is a category mistake.[5] Transitioning from one ethical context to another thus clearly involves replacing an entire epistemic and normative framework—a paradigm shift that at first glance appears to come from out of the blue.

When Marx thus claims that "from the standpoint of a higher socioeconomic formation, the private property of particular individuals in the earth will appear just as tasteless as the private property of one man in other men," he means that today, private ownership of the earth seems completely unproblematic and inevitable. Incapable of imagining any other relationship to the earth, it doesn't occur to us that there might be a problem here. Yet there may come another time and a *different social order* in which the fundamental understanding (and fundamental consensus) that constitutes our moral sense will have changed, just as it has already changed with respect to owning human beings. The institution of private property (in the earth) will then strike us as unseemly and repulsive, and we will struggle to understand how anyone could ever have treated the earth in this way. Thus understood, the adjective "tasteless" points to the *background conditions of a society's ethical life*, or its proto-values.[6] It points, that is, to the fundamental social epistemology and social ontology that make certain institutions and practices possible or impossible, conceivable or inconceivable, in the first place.

Perhaps we can only begin to appreciate how radical the accomplished break in relation to owning humans was—for Egon Flaig, the abolition of slavery amounts to the "most profound rupture in human history"—when we recall the moral obliviousness toward slavery, including in its cruelest excesses, shown even by individuals who in other respects possessed a refined moral sensibility.[7] Elizabeth Anderson cites a striking example of such a dramatic shift in moral convictions. She describes the captain of an African slave ship who delivered thousands of slaves to their fate and thought nothing of torturing his human cargo when he suspected them of plotting an insurrection. Yet this same captain saw himself doing God's work, led his crew in regular prayer, and kept a meticulous record of his own moral failings such as his habit of swearing.[8] From the perspective of a moral epistemology, this is an extraordinary testimony. The captain was no sociopath, no unfeeling monster bereft of a moral compass, but a God-fearing, morally sensitive Christian.[9] How are we to understand such a gap in moral perceptions? How could he have been so unresponsive to the torments of those he oppressed that they never even troubled his conscience? I am interested here less in individual psychology than in the social context in which this occurred. How should we conceptualize the transition from a moral frame of reference in which slavery comes across as perfectly natural and morally neutral to one in which it is a shocking moral scandal?[10]

Transformation as gestalt switch?

There is much to suggest that such a transformative process is not triggered (solely) by a purely rationally motivated change in convictions. As we have seen, what has happened here is more aptly described as a paradigm shift from intelligibility to unintelligibility than as a refutation within the sphere of the intelligible. What has changed is not how this or that practice is evaluated but, as in the Marx quote discussed above, what is thinkable and unthinkable— that is, the whole gamut of what is normatively up for debate: the frame of reference of moral judgments. We have here what Alasdair MacIntyre calls an "epistemological crisis": a state in which the interpretive framework of a social order itself plunges into crisis, necessitating a transformation of that very framework.[11]

There is thus something in the phenomenology of our moral experience that sometimes—especially in the case of glaring moral evils—confronts us with changes that initially present themselves as a kind of gestalt switch, like the famous rabbit-duck illusion.[12] Once the change in moral stance has been fully embraced, perceiving the same situation any other way must seem unimaginable. No discernible path then leads from here back to there. The associated feelings and attitudes become internalized to the point where they align, in a manner reminiscent of Schiller, with the spontaneous inclinations of our senses.[13] A "new normal" is established; something different from before is now taken for granted. Marx's use of the word "tasteless," with its aesthetic associations, gains plausibility in this respect.

Depth dynamic and reaction

Should we then follow Richard Rorty, who has described the path "from there to here" as one for which there is no rational basis, recommending that it be traversed through a "sentimental education" that trains the imaginative faculty?[14] The idea of an abrupt paradigm shift unmediated by reason is clearly not the position endorsed by Marx, neither in how it explains the phenomenon nor in terms of the strategies it offers for combating moral wrongs. As the above quote shows, Marx joins Rorty in distinguishing between two radically different standpoints: the "standpoint of a higher socioeconomic formation," in which private ownership of the earth has become unthinkable ("tasteless"), and the previous standpoint, from which it was still conceivable. These two perspectives are so radically different that what has become unthinkable from one seems perfectly normal from the other, and vice versa. For Marx, too, the transition from one perspective to the other does not proceed by means of a step-by-step insight into normative arguments. In contrast to the idea of a sudden gestalt switch, however, he describes a rational transition with an internal logic. The decisive point in Marx's description of the transformation in question is accordingly not the apparent disconnect between the two moral standpoints. It is instead that the relevant changes do not take place in the sphere of moral beliefs but in the "socioeconomic formations" that underlie moral judgments, including those pertaining to ownership of the earth or human beings.

What is going on here? Marx first historicizes the unthinkability of the transition by stating that the described practices and institutions present themselves as "tasteless" from the standpoint of a "higher," historically more advanced economic formation. He grasps the movement from the thinkable and self-evident to the unthinkable as one element in a broader sociohistorical development. In doing so, he assumes that such a transition from one socioeconomic formation to the next is not a clean break but a transformation that occurs for understandable reasons and in accordance with its own internal logic.

From this historical perspective, what was once thinkable appears as having somehow outlived its purpose, the abolition of such a practice as a "necessary and timely" step.[15] However radical the gestalt switch depicted above may be, it has a prehistory and a trajectory; it is the expression or outcome of a historical development that must be understood in its logic if the switch itself is to be understood. This is also how we should read the observation that provides this chapter with its epigraph: revolutionary changes occur when "within the old society the elements of a new one have been created." Marx materializes this shift, arguing that the change in question can be reconstructed based on the logic of a socioeconomic development. The economic management of material problems in life is thus the principal agent of change, as it were. Driven by the development of productive forces, the relations of production change along with our entire living conditions, including the norms that guide them.

Marx therefore solves the problem of the transition from one moral order to another by distinguishing between two levels: a deep level of economic-material transformation, governed by a comprehensible logic, which instigates the change in our normative standpoint, and a second, higher level where this change in standpoint takes the form of a shift in moral attitudes. What at first glance looks like an abrupt gestalt switch—from taken-for-granted to tasteless—can only appear as such if this depth dimension is ignored or misunderstood. Seen in this way, the idea that we are dealing here with a gestalt switch of the rabbit-duck kind itself proves to be an optical illusion. To be more precise, it is a perspective distorted through only looking at the surface of changed moral attitudes. (I will have more to say below about the problematic nature of this surface-depth distinction.)

Morality as ideology

To contrast the Marx-inspired position I have presented here once again with Rorty's, neither perspective views the process of radical moral change as an argument-driven revision of our moral beliefs in which we convince ourselves of the untenability of our previous positions and the rightness of our new ones. Rorty reaches this conclusion from a less cognitivist view of how moral attitudes are formed, while for Marx, the driving force behind the change is not even to be found in debate about moral ideas. Rorty remains an idealist in this respect, notwithstanding his provocative disdain for cognitivist moral theories. As we have seen, the social dynamic thematized by Marx, far from stemming from a genuine transformation in our moral sensibility and normative convictions, has its roots in what he calls the "development of the forces of production." These encompass whatever society needs to ensure its material reproduction: natural, technical, logistical, and intellectual-scientific resources as well as human labor. In Marx's view, a society's normative convictions have no dynamic of their own; they do not undergo any genuine, autonomous development. Conceived as "ideology," morality has "no history," as he says.[16] This does not mean that it does not change, only that it does not change of its own accord or according to an inherent dynamic. More precisely, it has no history *of its own*. The "contention over moral principles" referred to by Anderson would then not itself be the engine or catalyst of changes in our moral convictions.[17] On the contrary, it is always reactive: new norms do not emerge primarily from dissatisfaction with old norms but respond to developments transpiring at the deep, dynamic level described above. But this means—to put it bluntly—that there is no such thing as morality as an independent phenomenon. Moral or normative progress itself turns out to be the mere reflection of underlying social and economic changes, even if it serves the important ideological function of legitimating, maintaining, and buttressing the relevant social and economic institutions.

To avoid any misunderstandings at this stage, let me state that I consider the orthodox historical-materialist narrative I have sketched here to be inadequate for several reasons.[18] As the vast majority of post-Marxists and even Marx himself noted, the base-superstructure model at work here is too deterministic, too narrow, and too one-sided to capture the complex network of mutual influences and interdependences between economic, social, cultural, and political practices that confronts us here. If I nonetheless invoke this theory, it is because it still has something to teach us about conceptualizing social change. Marx draws our attention to a point that is all too often neglected in philosophical discussions today: changes in our moral imagination are not simply endogenous phenomena but arise and solidify in tandem with other social changes. What changes is thus nothing less than an entire "social formation," as Marx calls it. There is no need for us to join him in opposing a "higher" social formation to a putatively lower one, or in mapping such a formation along a simple distinction between surface and depth (or base and superstructure). Marx is asking the right question, even if his answer needs revising from today's point of view.[19]

From our first, Marx-inspired run-up to the question of how moral convictions are transformed, we thus arrive at an initial, deliberately open-ended and tentative thesis about the dynamic of moral progress, namely that moral progress does not stand on its own, and the progress we think we can detect with regard to moral questions, narrowly conceived, is embedded in and reliant on social frameworks and background conditions. The change in our evaluation of institutions and practices described as moral progress does not result from a free-floating moral insight or a solitary engagement of moral empathy. It is the effect of a sea change in entire social formations, a shift in surrounding or neighboring practices and the interpretive horizon within which the morally relevant practices and convictions in question have taken shape and come to prevail. Translated into Hegelian terms, morality is always rooted in *ethical life*—that is, in the historically specific practices and institutions in which we lead our social lives—and it is on this level that changes take place.

3.2 Relations of fit: The embedding of moral convictions in ethical life

Moral progress, I contend, occurs neither as an abrupt gestalt switch nor as a mere process of moral purification. It emerges from changing background conditions, from adjacent practices and institutions that gradually reshape and transform the environment of morally relevant practice until the latter appears in a new light. This thesis can be clarified through an example already touched on in Chapter 1, that of spousal rape. In Germany, rape was legally defined until 1997 as an "extramarital act," suggesting that there could be no rape within marriage or that nonconsensual sex within marriage did not count as rape. When it came into force, this statute was in line with other provisions of family law, such as the husband's right to control his wife's property and to terminate her employment contract of his own accord.[20] Such provisions may seem bizarre from today's perspective, yet they remained the law of the land until 1953, at least in West Germany. They went hand in hand with a social arrangement in which wives were typically economically dependent on their husbands. From the general "duty to obey" that defined the wife's role in this notion of wedlock, it was only a small step to a specifically sexual form of subordination. Indeed, a "refusal to perform conjugal duties" was widely (and institutionally) recognized as constituting grounds for divorce.

All this was informed by a seemingly innocuous interpretation of marriage as an intimate, divinely ordained covenant or "organic unit."[21] The idea of intimacy at work here may explain the much-invoked fear of the "prosecutor under the marriage bed," a fear which has at times seemed to overshadow abhorrence at the acts of violence committed between the sheets.[22] Finally, an essentializing conception of male and female sexuality which saw the latter in terms of passive endurance and submission may also have contributed to the coercive violation of the wife's sexual integrity being construed as a variant of a *sexual relationship* rather than as a form of (sexualized) *violence*.[23]

The fact that it was (and still is) so difficult to invalidate marriage as a relationship of proprietorial dominance and to punish by law the acts of violence perpetrated in its name reflects a peculiarly stubborn duality in the institution and idea of marriage. While the notion of marriage as an intimate partnership stands opposed to a legalistic conception, in practice it involves relations of power and dominance. The "master of the house" was just that: a master. This was the challenge faced by the women's movement, and it could only be successful in this regard because it broadly thematized the dimension addressed here rather than simply denouncing what was morally offensive in the narrower sense in the patriarchal organization of gender relations, from sexuality to domestic arrangements that confined women to the home.

Similar contextual factors can be identified for the institution of slavery and for the infliction of violence—mostly physical but also psychological—on children. Slavery in its various forms can be placed on a continuum with other practices of social domination and racist exclusion, as well as with other forms of unfree labor and social exchange relations. Similarly, violence in education and other practices of "poisonous pedagogy" become intelligible only when viewed in connection with associated ideas of childhood and the nature of children.[24] These assume children to be essentially wild, untamed creatures who must be civilized and disciplined for their own good through the appropriate educational methods. The acceptance of violence in childrearing is further linked to how society approaches corporal punishment in general as well as particular ideas about paternal authority, which in turn are bound up with social concepts of unconditional obedience to authority. As with spousal rape, it is only against such a nexus of intertwined practices and interpretations that corporal punishment can be accepted as a legitimate educational measure, or even as an expression of parental care and love, not just as brute force.[25]

Mismatches and disrupted relations of fit

If normalization is the condition for the consolidation of such practices, then moral change—the modification or repudiation of such practices—occurs, conversely, when such a nexus is destabilized and/or reconfigured. In other words, whether the beating of children or spousal rape arouses moral indignation is linked to shifts and slippages in an entire network of practices. Moral change is then brought about not least by the fact that the background conditions and practical consequences of widely held moral convictions are no longer the same. This can happen, for example, when traditional relations of fit erode, becoming unstable and vulnerable to attack. Practices and interpretations that previously cohered seamlessly now misalign or contradict each other. New practices and new techniques are added to an ensemble of practices and interpretations; the conditions under which these are deployed and the interpretations that accompany them change. Some practices (still) fit into the ensemble while other, new additions seem to shatter it. In some cases, an entire nexus or ensemble of social practices is completely or partially disrupted. The old must then bow out. The new is sometimes already waiting in the wings, sometimes not; or it is there but hard to make out.

As is well documented, temporary shifts in gender relations occurred during the Second World War and in the immediate postwar period as women took on jobs that had previously been monopolized by men and assumed sole responsibility for managing and maintaining family life.[26] But even setting aside such dramatic caesuras, the labor market (and society at large) has undergone such far-reaching change since then that the claim that the woman's place is in the home and that she owes her husband fealty as her lord and master has lost all credibility. It is certainly no longer the only option. Such ideas, like the husband's right to control his wife's property and terminate her employment contract, now seem hopelessly outdated.

Even apparently inconspicuous technological inventions can precipitate social and moral change. In this respect, the television series *Downton Abbey* tells a story of social progress, even if it tends to romanticize working conditions in aristocratic households.[27]

The plot cleverly shows how love, war, the wireless, telephone, and typewriter combine with inefficient aristocratic farming methods and emerging emancipatory movements to create a transformational dynamic that progressively undermines the traditional lifestyle of the British aristocracy, ultimately dooming it to extinction. A striking example of the materiality of this change is the typewriter secretly acquired by the housemaid Gwen, revealed to the assembled downstairs staff as an icon of the new age.[28] The typewriter symbolizes the promise of more highly qualified paid work freed from the comprehensive personal dependency and drudgery of domestic service—a promise that is fulfilled when Gwen is offered a secretarial position. Smuggled into the enclave of an old-fashioned, feudally preserved way of life, these elements of a new age corrode it from within. We sense this when the Earl's family rise awkwardly from their chairs in front of the newly installed wireless set upon hearing the King's voice. The slight hesitation with which they perform the gesture, since no one seems to know whether they ought to pay homage to the crackling royal voice broadcast into their sitting room, hints that the traditional social order may soon become a casualty of the newfangled technology.

But it is not just these tangible technical innovations that intrude here upon a familiar repertoire of social practices. Just as the aristocratic form of life is undermined by technological developments, so too it proves ill-equipped to deal with the social upheavals brought about by the First World War, including more liberal values and the much-invoked leveling effect of the camaraderie between officers and common soldiers born of their shared experience in the trenches. The scandalously inappropriate love affair between one of the daughters of the house and the socialist, Irish Catholic chauffeur—a classic *mésalliance* from the perspective of tradition—is a well-worn literary trope about the power of erotic attraction and romantic love to defy social conventions. Yet it is not just the all-conquering romantic ideal of love that challenges the aristocratic, genealogical-reproductive conception of marriage here. It is not by chance that the suitor happens to be a politically radical chauffeur, hence a figure who embodies access to a brave new world of both technology and ideas.

Unintended connections

Moral progress is then sometimes the result of a complex chain of intended and unintended actions.[29] Changes in *one* complex of practices—the invention of the typewriter, the birth control pill, or gunpowder—can spill over into other areas, without these changes being explicitly intended or even foreseen. In his book on "moral revolutions," Kwame Anthony Appiah has argued that the appreciation for labor that emerged with the bourgeois world in the nineteenth century helped to foster solidarity between the newly self-aware working classes and the abolitionist movement.[30] This was certainly galvanized by moral indignation at the cruelty and inhumanity of slavery as well as by a broadly conceived class solidarity. But it was also fueled by protest against the callous disregard for work expressed in slavery, which stood at odds with the dignity labor was accorded in early bourgeois society. Appiah's general thesis is that moral revolutions do not just have to do with changing perceptions of moral duties; they are embedded in a more comprehensive ethos, the binding yet variable "honor code" of a given society and time.

From there, it is only a small step to the even more complex picture I would like to draw. Appiah's reference to shifts in ethos raises the question of how and why the honor code and the ethos of a society in general changes. In the case of working-class opposition to slavery, how did labor come to be reevaluated? An entire network of social and economic factors played a part, ranging from the increasing social irrelevance of the nobility and the ideal of chivalry to changes in the technical conditions of labor, new requirements for workplace cooperation, new conditions for the division of labor, and the emergence of a collective class consciousness on the part of the proletariat. If the nobility's loss of social significance (to take up one of these possible threads) is in turn multifactorial and already begins with the invention of gunpowder, which made the knights' military virtues superfluous, then an admittedly rather simplistic narrative could be sketched that has the invention of gunpowder leading—through many twists and turns—to the abolition of slavery.[31] Similarly, a case could be made that the inventor of the typewriter contributed to the criminalization of spousal rape. Other such plots are conceivable.

To focus on just one aspect of this dynamic of social change: the threads that can be spun here are sometimes the unintended side effects of actions undertaken with other ends in mind. Change in one area (the invention of the typewriter) can bring about social change of a completely different kind (opportunities for modern women to lead a more independent lifestyle). Some social developments thus come about inadvertently, without any of the parties involved having necessarily intended them. These can then serve, however, as springboards for those advocating a certain direction of social change—in our examples, pioneers of female emancipation, slaves and their supporters campaigning for the abolition of slavery, or emancipatory movements targeting the authoritarian family and its childrearing practices. They can provide opportunities for the corresponding social movements to forge alliances and take action. Progress is then change within change.[32]

3.3 The temporal core of morality

Having claimed in this chapter that a change in a society's moral convictions only takes place when it is not *just* moral convictions that change, and that moral progress accordingly does not unfold autonomously, I am now in a position to explain this position further and outline some of its consequences.

Embedding relationships and interdependencies

Let us first take another look at the embedding relationships and interdependencies that my description has brought to light:

(1) *The interweaving of moral and ethical norms.* As we saw above, "contention over moral principles" in the narrow sense is embedded in debate about other questions concerning how we should lead our lives, as well as in the institutions and practices in which these principles are realized.[33] The opportunity to end violence against children or in marriage—or rather, to prohibit it, and thereby create the conditions for ending it in the first place, however arduous this project remains in view of the systemic obstacles and setbacks that continue to dog it—arises when the practices and institutions of family life in general change along with the norms that govern them. These changes in the ethical fabric of familial relationships, gender relations, and educational ethos may not be moral questions in the narrow sense.[34] But they have consequences for what is deemed morally (im)permissible and for what is possible in terms of moral renewal. Morality, as any good Hegelian would say, is based in ethical life. More narrowly moral questions are a part of ethical life: they are anchored in an ethical nexus of practice and cannot be categorically separated from it.[35]

(2) *The entanglement of normative and non-normative beliefs.* If moral norms in the narrow sense are embedded in ethical norms, normative questions as a whole are interwoven with beliefs that are not normative at first glance or in any narrow sense. The "historical processes of contention over moral principles [that] lead groups to change their moral convic-

tions" are tied up with how we see the world.[36] Normative practices do not just change because how we think we *ought* to act (in the sense of practical reason) changes; they also change because of changes in our knowledge of the world, our view of the world, our understanding of how the world *is*. More than normative arguments are therefore needed to denounce moral outrages. Criticism of "poisonous pedagogy" draws not just on a changed understanding of our moral obligations but also on a changed idea of what children are, what they need, and what childhood is.[37] Or to take a very different example: famously, no "contention" within society did more to erode traditional authority than that provoked by the Copernican reform. It could even be argued that debates aimed at overthrowing traditional sources of authority first became possible on the basis of this reform.

To avoid any misunderstandings, I am not suggesting here that a norm-free world, the world *as it is*, can be opposed to the world of norms, the world *as it should be*.[38] The key point is rather that the two cannot be separated: our idea of what the world is and our idea of how it should be and how we should relate to it. The normative is bound up with the epistemic.[39] If our view of the world is always already evaluative, then new understandings of the world and ourselves will give rise to new knowledge, just as, conversely, this knowledge will influence how we understand the world and ourselves.

(3) *The embedding of practices and beliefs in material resources.* Our practices (and the beliefs that accompany and legitimate them) are embedded in material resources; indeed, they are first made possible by such resources and build up around them. Material resources enable and generate patterns of behavior that can in turn change the resources at our disposal. Not only is a world populated by computers and smartphones different from one with books and plows. The same is true of

the people who use such implements, and in whom the actions they make possible (but also necessitate) are inscribed.[40] They are different, too, depending on whether they go around using smartphones and computers or books and plows. We should not imagine this process in overly concrete terms: the resources in question primarily create relationships (with ourselves, with the world, with others). The steam engine is not some arbitrary, stand-alone artifact. Because of it, labor arrangements were reorganized and industrialized on a massive scale, with the familiar consequences: factory work, urbanization, separation of the workplace from the household sphere, intensified global exchange, and so on. Similarly, the smartphone is not just an inert object; it actively shapes users' relationships with the world, with others, and with themselves.

(4) *The entanglement of beliefs and practices.* From the perspective adopted here, beliefs and practices are closely intertwined. Beliefs are embedded in practices, practices in beliefs. Beliefs (normative or otherwise) are not immaculately conceived in some practice-free zone of values or ideas. As interpretations rooted in a real-world context, they are interwoven with practices and change alongside them.

It is not as if ideas change first and *then* practices; rather, the two go hand in hand. It is always a raft of ideas, practical changes, and (their) interpretations that are swept along by change and at the same time constitute that change. Sometimes one is reminded of Pascal's injunction: "Kneel down, move your lips in prayer, and you will believe."[41] Sometimes, however, it is the other way around: you believe, and so you kneel down. Sometimes newly emerging interpretations lead to practical changes or new practices, while at others, practical changes lead to new interpretations. We are almost always dealing with dynamics that cannot easily be disentangled into their individual elements.

Morality as a reflection of living conditions

What follows from these entanglements and embedding relationships? In my view, they make for a stronger, systematically more
important argument than the presumably uncontroversial, essentially methodological point that morally relevant changes depend
empirically on what Habermas calls "accommodating forms of
life." The term "embedding" may even be misleading here, suggesting a constancy in what is embedded that is belied by the
changes undergone on both sides through their interweaving. If we
accept this argument, then we can see that the approach to the
question of moral progress ventured here has consequences for
how we understand morality even as it builds on a certain understanding of morality. Roughly speaking, my position accords with
a pragmatist position that sees morality as a reflection of living
conditions. According to this position, moral or ethical norms help
us come to grips with problems in life and emerge in response to
such problems. Morality is then a system of rules for regulating and
stabilizing our coexistence, as Émile Durkheim would also argue
from a normative-functionalist perspective. Debate over moral
principles is accordingly (with Dewey) an occasion for reflecting
on, and working out solutions to, the problems that arise from
living together, from the social cooperation on which human life
depends.

Once we take this view, however, an image of moral principles
where fixed normative principles come to prevail in an ever-
changing world—the default deontological position—is no longer
plausible. Principles themselves change as the world does, if for no
other reason than that they are continually faced with new tasks.
Elizabeth Anderson deftly sketches this view with reference to
Dewey:

> We advance moral principles to solve recurring problems in our social
> lives. When circumstances change, those principles may no longer

solve these problems, or new problems may arise for which they are
unequipped. This may trigger fresh moral inquiry, a search for new
principles . . . .[42]

The normative foundations of our social lives (and also morality)
thus have a temporal core. If moral progress is encompassed, in the
way I have just outlined, by progress in ethical life and "living conditions" as well as our understanding of these things as a whole,
then principles change with living conditions and these changes,
conversely, have a normative core. In contrast to a two-worlds
theory of practical reason, I would contend that norms, including
moral norms, are not ultimate principles (that is, categorical principles that apply in all possible worlds). In Anderson's words, "in
place of an ultimate principle, pragmatism offers methods for improving our moral norms and principles."[43] Morality as a whole
then presents itself (to borrow an idea from Philippa Foot) as a
system of "hypothetical imperatives" whose validity cannot be determined absolutely—categorically—but stems from their role in
facilitating social cooperation and overcoming the problems that
arise from living together.[44] We could call this a "functionalist account of morality" in which "the moral norms that bind us are ultimately constructed by members of social groups as part of an
ongoing attempt to figure out a way of living together."[45] This has
consequences for the question of genesis and validity touched on
above.

In a trivial sense that would also be accepted by Kantians, moral
progress is based empirically and in its genesis on "accommodating"
background conditions in the lifeworld. The pragmatist-functionalist
account of morality as rooted in living conditions, however, concerns
not just the genesis of such progress but also its validity. (It is at this
point, incidentally, that the claim made in Chapter 1 for the primacy
of progress over the good is redeemed.) This is because moral principles in the narrow sense, insofar as they are based in an ethical and

material nexus of practice, have a history that is normatively meaningful as the history of ever-improving (or ever-worsening) attempts to find solutions to problems arising in the social sphere. Moral progress is then not progress *toward* morality, toward the right thing to do, but progress *in* morality. In its entanglement with ethical life, morality itself has a temporal core. This means that the development of the norms in question is a historical-social process that, instead of opening the field for moral relativism, has a normative significance of its own.

The position sketched here has a further corollary: the question of *how* we organize our lives together, and the norms that guide us in doing so, cannot be neatly separated from the question of *what* we are organizing, the basis—including the material basis—on which we shape our lives together and the resources and capabilities we draw on in producing and reproducing our lives.[46]

If moral progress therefore stands in the context of comprehensive changes in many different areas of life, it does not follow that there is any "unbreakable chain" or direct causal relationship between individual processes of social change, as assumed by philosophers of progress in the eighteenth and nineteenth centuries. The chain is perhaps more brittle than unbreakable, and it may not always be a chain, but sometimes a ball of twine with many loose threads. The sharp distinction mentioned in the Introduction between technoscientific progress and the ethical, moral, or political advances that affect how we live our lives then proves as untenable as the idea that social progress occurs solely at the level of changes in people's minds.

How exactly all these factors interact remains unclear, however. In the next section, a conceptual intermezzo, I would like to explicate the theoretical terminology that has already partly informed my discussion. With its help, I will then continue exploring this interaction and the ways in which forms of life are transformed as a result.

3.4 Conceptual intermezzo: Forms of life as inert ensembles of practices

It has emerged from my account so far that the site of the changes grouped under the collective singular "(social) progress" is the ensemble of social practices and institutions I call "forms of life." But what is meant by "forms of life" here?[47] And how can they change?

Forms of life are the forms in which a society (re)produces its material and cultural life. I take them to refer to culturally shaped "orders of human coexistence."[48] They are an "ensemble of practices and orientations."[49] But also included are their institutional manifestations and materializations. As collective formations of human life, they embrace its constituent economic, cultural, social, and political practices. In addition to forms of social intercourse, practically and institutionally embodied norms of social interaction, and the organization of the social division of labor, these include technical skills as well as the materials or resources we work with and on. In referring to forms of life, I therefore do not mean to oppose "culture" to the material, economic, or political aspects of the nexus of society.[50]

The conceptualization I am proposing can be summed up as follows: *forms of life are inert ensembles of social practices*. To clarify what this means exactly, it is worth breaking down this definition into its elements: the concept of (social) *practices*, the claim that they relate to each other as an *ensemble*, and the suggestion that this ensemble is *inert*.

(1) *Social practices* in different aggregate states are the building blocks of forms of life, as it were.[51] They are ways of doing something or making something happen. They involve dealing with others, the material world, or with oneself—these dimensions being interwoven in multiple ways. A dinner party or

game of hide-and-seek is no less a social practice than going shopping, taking an exam, organizing a demonstration, or bringing in the harvest. Practices are sequences of individual actions that are more or less complex and comprehensive and more or less habitualized. They are to some extent binding and they are repetitive: something performed once and once only or by a single human being is not a practice. Practices are social *per se* because they can only exist and be understood against the backdrop of socially constituted spaces of meaning and have social functions, not because they relate exclusively to social cooperation in a more limited sense. Hence, it is not just a communal game of football but also the solitary actions of cooking dinner for one, applying makeup in front of a mirror, or meditating in the wilderness that are social practices. These practices draw on socially established meanings and play out in a socially constructed space of meaning. Practices are patterns of action that allow us to act in the first place and, at the same time, must be produced and continually actualized through our activity. Because such patterns are norm-governed and hence contain the conditions for their own realization, they set limits to our actions. (If I do not at least make an effort to hide, I cannot legitimately be said to participate in the practice of playing hide-and-seek.) These patterns also, however, first make our actions possible. (Without the corresponding norms, there would be no game.) In addition, three specific aspects should be pointed out in our context.[52]

First, insofar as they contain an element of habit, practices are not just based on deliberate—that is, intentional actions. To a certain extent, and as long as they are not disrupted or confronted with problems, practices are based on implicit rather than explicit knowledge. Next, practices are not "bare facts": they have to be understood and interpreted as something. From the mere fact that someone is standing behind a tree, I cannot yet tell whether they are a wanted fugitive or playing hide-and-seek. To understand hiding behind a tree as a move in a game, I need additional information. I have to know the game called hide-and-seek (including its rules) and I have to be able to identify it in what I'm seeing. Moreover, by being able to understand their action as part of a game, I also implicitly understand how it relates to other practices and their interpretations. I then understand the concept or scheme of interpretation "game" (in contrast to "work") and possibly the concept of childhood as opposed to adulthood, and much more. Practices can thus only be understood against an interpretive horizon that encompasses other practices and interpretations.

Third, it is important to bear in mind the normativity specific to practices. If our participation in a particular practice is oriented to the expectations that go along with it, then we are not dealing here with arbitrary or purely conventional agreements. Practices are organized around the key idea of fulfilling the practice in question. Whoever doesn't bother hiding hasn't understood the game; if someone shows no inclination to take down products from the shelves and put them in the shopping trolley but just strolls aimlessly around the supermarket, this doesn't count as shopping. Practices have an inherent *telos* or end. They are directed at a goal that can be achieved through them. Participating in a practice—genuinely partaking in it—thus presupposes that one is acting with its end and the internal criteria for realizing that end in mind. This applies even if several goals can be pursued simultaneously through a certain practice, which is accordingly overdetermined.

(2) What I call *inertia* in describing forms of life as inert ensembles of social practices has several features. Forms of life contain sedimented elements, habits, and other practical components

that are not readily accessible, explicit, or transparent in all respects. But they also contain dimensions of historical tradition and material prerequisites that shape the available patterns of action and can inhibit their dynamics. Forms of life thus move in an intermediate space between accessibility and inaccessibility. Although they are the results of human action, it is not the case that they are (always) fluid, accessible, or even transparent in their being made. They are the result of our activity, but also what makes such activity possible; they are the result of our deeds, but also the pattern of action and interpretation that shapes such deeds. Accordingly, forms of life can be neither imposed nor modified by fiat. Once we have entered a form of life, we do not relate to it as if it were a completely transparent and selectable bundle of options.

(3) Understanding forms of life as *ensembles* of practices is especially important for the line of questioning pursued in this chapter. First of all, a single practice does not yet constitute a form of life. Going shopping and playing hide-and-seek are not themselves forms of life, although they may be elements of one. As we have seen, an individual practice can first be understood against the backdrop of a form of life, a nexus of practices and interpretations; indeed, in many cases it is possible only within such a nexus of interrelated practices. What we could call a form of life is thus made up of various practices. However, these are not a jumble of otherwise unrelated elements; they enter into a constellation, an ensemble from which they draw their respective content even as they bestow on the ensemble its defining characteristics. The corresponding practices work together in coordinated fashion to realize the goals associated with a nexus of practices, and their meaning can change depending on the constellation of practices in effect in the ensemble in question.

How practices relate to each other within a form of life can vary greatly. In some but not all cases, their interconnection is evidently based on a social division of labor. The practice of supermarket shopping, for example, is the end point in a whole series of other practices that first make it possible. It comprises a number of steps, from the practices and resources that go into producing the goods offered for sale via the complicated logistics involved in their distribution to stacking them on the supermarket shelves. In an economy based on a strict division of labor, these steps are in turn made possible by various other institutions, such as a certain education system or a certain organization of family reproductive work. If many practices first derive their meaning and their conditions of possibility from being embedded in such a nexus— hence, if the good and the purpose that a practice is supposed to realize cannot be realized in it alone—then forms of life turn out to be structured ensembles in which complex goods or purposes are pursued.

Some practices cannot easily be detached from their nexus because the existence of other practices depends on them. If no one is there to stack the shelves and if there is nothing to be stacked, all connecting practices and ultimately the reproduction of the form of life will be put at risk. Readers of *The Last Man Alive*, Alexander Sutherland Neill's seminal novel of antiauthoritarian education, will recall the moment when the children who have escaped the green cloud that turns everyone else into stone realize that their now unrestricted access to supermarkets and toy shops will be of no use to them in the long run.[53]

Characterizing forms of life as "ensembles of practices" further means that the associated nexus is not set in stone and allows for weaker connections. Individual practices can continue to exist separately from the rest, or they can be replaced by functional equivalents. Relations between practices that together make up the ensemble of a form of life can thus be configured in a variety of ways; sometimes the nexus is more

tightly woven, other times more loosely. Some clusters within
a form of life are closely and functionally integrated; others
may fit together in a looser, less specific sense but cannot
easily be imagined in isolation from each other, or from the
form of life in general. Some practices are incidental; others
are nodal points (to stick with the image of a network).

Referring to forms of life as *ensembles* of practices also
means refining the notion of societies as organisms.[54] Whereas
the organism metaphor implies strict, binding, unequivocal relations and functions, that of the ensemble is more flexible. An
ensemble—let us take a large symphony orchestra—consists
of interrelated parts and sub-functions that can only produce
the desired sound or create a complex dynamic when they
work together. Within the ensemble, however, different relationships assume importance depending on the piece being
played. Some voices reinforce each other (the violin section),
others complement each other or pass the melody around like
a baton in a relay race. There are functional equivalents for
some parts—a gloomy, foreboding dark tone can be produced
with double basses or using brass or percussion; bright voices
can be represented by violins or flutes—but not for others.
There are passing resemblances here to an organism, and we
do indeed sometimes describe an orchestra playing "organi-
cally" or liken it to a single living, breathing animal. The underlying assumptions are not, however, as strong or binding as
those associated with an organism. While the heart has only
one function, to pump blood, the cello can fulfill different
functions in different constellations. The functions are more
fluid and variable. Yet here, too, if a single practice changes,
the nexus (often) changes as well. And conversely, one has to
change the nexus—the ensemble and the social structure—to
change the individual practice.

3.5 "Keeping pace": A web of interrelationships

This brings me back to the question of the interactions and inter-relationships between different complexes of practices and convictions. My thesis in this section is that, in light of the embedding relationships and interdependencies outlined above, we can gain a picture of the complex interrelationships between diverse spheres of practice which goes beyond the simplistic image of a surface controlled from below (the economic base). An understanding of the ensemble character of social practices will allow us to understand them as multiple dynamics that relate to and influence each other in their very autonomy and distinctiveness.

If, as I have been arguing, moral progress takes place in the broader context of social change, hence in situations in which ethical, technological, and cultural practices change or become obsolete alongside habitual moral judgments and institutions, then moral progress does not unfold *endogenously* or autonomously. But I would also claim that it is not entirely *exogenous* either. Starting out from a network of diverse practices and beliefs with a distinct developmental logic of its own, the situation is such that normative changes are enabled and sometimes triggered, but not determined, by non-normative changes. We should not assume that moral—or, more generally, *normative*—beliefs develop completely autonomously to drive social development, nor should we view them as developing purely reactively, as mere expressions or "reflections" of non-normative dynamics. For as unthinkable as female emancipation may be without the pill and the typewriter, the pill and the typewriter did not emancipate women all by themselves.

As quoted in the epigraph to this chapter, Marx thinks "that the dissolution of the old ideas keeps even pace with the dissolution of the old living conditions." In my view, this should not be taken to mean that living conditions are the pacemaker setting the direction, rhythm, and speed of the march, while ideas merely follow and react. If ideas are the result of living conditions, then conversely, living conditions are the result of ideas. As explained above, such practices are always already interpreted, which also means that they are normatively interpreted practices; they are what they are against the background of a normatively imbued interpretive horizon. Insofar as normative interpretations and beliefs are embedded in the practices that constitute living conditions, there can be no clear dichotomy between ideas and living conditions. Ideas and living conditions "keep pace" *with each other* in complex causal loops without either taking the front foot.

The image that emerges contradicts the Marxist thesis invoked above that ideology (or the set of normative beliefs that characterizes our living conditions) has "no history" and merely follows the dynamic of changing material living conditions (or the development of the forces of production). The spheres in question are each dynamic in their own right—they have their own dynamic and history—but are mutually enmeshed in this dynamic. They enable and influence each other, a concatenation of dynamics that are at once distinct and interrelated.

Overdetermined relations

Different strands of action from different areas of life—economic innovations, technical inventions, political events, changes in how people see themselves and relate to the world—come together when social transformations take place. On the one hand, these (sometimes very long) threads of development are interwoven in diverse, sometimes barely discernible ways. On the other hand, each dimension of social life—family, labor, technical innovations, political rule—has its own internal logic. I understand the processes at work here as problem-solving dynamics (and will return to this more explicitly in the next chapter). Such problem-solving dynamics can be found in relation to very different dimensions of our social existence; they are far from homogeneous and are not necessarily coordinated with each other. There is a problem-solving dynamic for technical inventions and innovations, but also for social customs, the organization of social rule, and the shape of political institutions. Technological developments, for example, lead to further such developments; they respond to preexisting needs and create new needs. They express developed capacities and help to foster new capacities.

For example, once computer technology had progressed to a certain level, it was only a matter of time before the computing machines initially commissioned by large governmental, scientific, and commercial organizations were made available for individual or even private use. The product differentiation this required could only be met by investing technical ingenuity and research funds into developing lighter, smaller, more efficient storage media. Or consider how access to the internet has become a social need serviced by a significant and growing part of our communications infrastructure. It is now taken for granted that we can tap into our private data, as well as a mind-bogglingly vast reservoir of information and other online resources, whenever and wherever we want. Every (artificial) limit to such unrestricted access must therefore present itself as a nuisance: a hurdle to be cleared or problem to be overcome. The line of development that led from early computing machines to the PC and laptop, as well as the parallel line of development from early telephony to the first rotary dial devices and networks to cell phones, thus has a certain internal logic that unfolds autonomously in some respects. In other respects, however, it is conditioned and heteronomously determined by other spheres of practice. There is thus an obvious link between, for example, the development of ICT and military technology (or the development of modern warfare).

Or consider a different dynamic. Ways of living together and their resulting normative claims can develop a logic of their own, such that socially accepted claims and possibilities can prompt further claims and usher in the renewal of the corresponding institutions and practices. To return to one of my prime examples, once the idea of love and voluntary commitment had established itself as the socially accepted principle of marriage, further claims and needs arose that evolved dynamically. As soon as the need to forge economic and social alliances between families from a similar class background no longer dictated partner choice, which therefore was now considered free, individualized, and above all driven by romantic considerations, the writing was on the wall for marriage restrictions based on religion. Since no one could be forcibly wed anymore, coercion within marriage also became increasingly inconsistent with the idea of marriage (which is not to say that it has ever disappeared). The shift from marriages of convenience to love matches, combined with the relaxation of the sociobiological imperative to reproduce within the constraints of wedlock, ultimately opened up the—still contested—possibility of accommodating homosexual partnerships within the institution of marriage, or indeed dissolving that institution altogether. But as we have seen, there are also non-normative framework conditions for this normative dynamic. Or rather: this normative dynamic interferes with non-normative dynamics.

We are dealing here with a complex nexus of interrelationships arising from the multifactorial mutual influence of diverse spheres of practices (or practices and beliefs), an intricately woven network of reciprocal dependencies, influences, effects, and connections of different kinds operating in different directions. These interference phenomena emerge as a sequence of inter(re)acting processes, events, and problems that is not systematically "directed" by a superordinate sphere and its logic. Might there be a hierarchy of practices? Are some practices more central than others, dominating or even "conducting" others, to reprise our orchestral analogy?[55] It may be assumed that there is no one identifiable socio-structural "change agent," no one bundle of practices that systematically determines all the rest. In different times and in different historical and social constellations there may, however, be various and variously dominant "anchor practices," particular complexes of practices that are indispensable for the reproduction of a specific form of life. Forms of life differ, among other things, in what these are and in which constellation they stand in relation to other practices.[56]

Mismatches and historical materialism

At this point, it is worth returning to the motif of "relations of fit" that I introduced earlier in broad outline and filling in some of the details by contrasting it with Marx's position. While I previously indicated how changes become possible once relations of fit between practices are disrupted, Marx draws on a quite distinct, more narrowly conceived relationship of fit to explain how its dissolution unleashes revolutionary but also less dramatic processes of social transformation. In a much-cited passage, he describes this pointedly—perhaps a little too pointedly.[57] It reads: "the hand mill yields a society with feudal lords, the steam mill a society with industrial capitalists."[58] Connections thus obtain between an entire complex of techniques, social practices, and forms of social organization, such that the hand mill befits a society with feudal lords and the steam mill befits a society with captains of industry. Yet Marx speaks here of one "yielding" the other. On one side, then, we have the hand mill along with its characteristic practices, technical skills, and associated labor regime (hence: the forces of production). On the other side is the feudal order with its social power relations and hierarchies, its distribution of economic and political influence, and its characteristic property relations and ways of life (hence: the relations of production). If we posit a functional relationship between the two sides, changes on one side—the invention of the steam engine, for example—can destabilize the other. The result is a constellation pushing for change: the maintenance of feudal relations under steam-age conditions then presents itself as a mismatch that leads to social upheaval and ultimately revolution (according to Marx). The development of the forces of production thus generates its own dynamic. Failing to keep pace, the relations of production lag behind, become dysfunctional, and—in a famous turn of phrase—become a "fetter" upon further development.[59]

As Louis Althusser noted, this is almost a caricature of the materialist view of history. Marx himself painted a much subtler picture, one that has since been retouched, revised, and reinterpreted in complex and wide-ranging ways from Althusser to Habermas (to name just two prominent examples). Particularly in analytical Marxism, the question of how the functional character of the relationship outlined here is to be understood has been the subject of much debate.[60]

My sketch of relations of fit, and the dynamic that transforms matches into misfits, is intended to serve merely as a foil for the expanded version of the mutual influences and interrelationships I have in mind. Everything depends on what we make of the mutually conditioning relationships which, in Marx's account, directly "yield" systemic change. Along with several other interpreters, I am interested in taking a more nuanced approach that explores how multiple practices interrelate in multiple ways in the dynamic ensemble of forms of life.

(1) *Reciprocity*. Rather than positing a one-sided, causal relationship between the development of the forces and relations of production, a moderated or expanded version of this relationship in my sense assumes their *reciprocal influence*. It is not just one side—the forces of production—that is intrinsically dynamic, with the other side reacting statically to its

propulsive charge; instead, both sides intersect and interact dynamically.

(2) *Normative permeation of the functional.* If the development of the forces of production is problem-driven, these problems also emerge in a normative and social environment. They become *particular* problems in a form that is always already normatively and "culturally" preconfigured, and they can only be solved in this form.

Taken together, these two theses can explain the extent to which advances in technology are always also social and cultural developments. If gunpowder was already known in ninth-century China but was mainly used for fireworks and ritual purposes, or if the steam engine was invented in classical antiquity but, instead of triggering an industrial revolution, remained confined to the sphere of entertainment and the theater, this shows that the pressure of economic problems is not solely responsible for unleashing the developmental dynamic of technical innovations.[61] This dynamic also owes a great deal to social contexts that embed such innovations in specific contexts of use and enable their further development and application in specific contexts of practice.

I said above that it took the typewriter to set in motion the emancipation of women, or gunpowder to delegitimize the nobility, but we can also grasp the stick from the other end. If female emancipation needed the typewriter, so too did the invention of the typewriter need female emancipation. Without the social changes that made it even conceivable for unmarried women to live on their own and work in an office instead of entering domestic service, a new type of employment relationship could not have crystallized around the typewriter, turning the male profession of private secretary into a female-dominated workforce of typists, stenographers, secretaries, and receptionists. Advances in technology can thus trigger social (and normative) changes, but conversely, they can also be set in motion or enabled by them.[62]

(3) *Dissolution of a strictly causal relationship.* Where an orthodox version of historical materialism assumes a strictly functional causal relationship between the forces and relations of production, the expanded version understands it as an *enabling relationship* and (in some cases) as an elective affinity in the Weberian sense. The change on one side is not the necessary and sufficient condition for the reaction on the other side but rather makes it possible, to put it in far more cautious terms. The hand mill does not "yield" feudal society in the sense that it forces it into being, nor does the steam engine "yield" bourgeois society; in each case, the former enables, suggests, or contributes to the persistence of the latter. To the extent that it calls for a reaction in the first place, however, since problems might arise from certain forms of non-reaction, we can discern here a (very weak) developmental logic.[63]

(4) *Functional equivalents.* Another way in which the version of functionalism I am proposing here has expanded beyond a narrowly conceived functional relationship—a functional necessity amenable to a purely functional explanation—is that it assumes the existence of *functional equivalents.* There is not just one possible reaction to an existing change or problem situation, but several. There is therefore variance within a spectrum of functionally "fit" adjustments. Put bluntly, the hand mill can "yield" feudal society, but also other forms of social organization, while the steam engine, even where it leads to an industrialized capitalism, can engender varieties of capitalism, or sometimes nothing at all. In other words, one and the same problem can have different functionally equivalent solutions, which in turn give rise to different follow-up problems and dynamics. As I will show in Chapter 4, these

dynamics can be described as *problem-solving processes* that
are both determinate and open-ended in nature.

The normative lodestar

Faced with these multiply interconnected dynamics, how can we
distinguish between progressive and non-progressive tendencies?
For Marx, the development of the forces of production was the
lodestar guiding the expansion of human capacities and opportunities for satisfying ever more ambitious needs. Once this is dis-
counted as a normative vector, the changes associated with it no
longer point to the true north of progress. After all, the transformations wrought by these forces are not progressive *per se*. As John
Dewey rightly remarks, "the forces which have brought about
complicated and extensive changes in the fabric of society do not of
themselves generate progress . . ."[64] This means two things: not
only do they not *automatically* generate progress, but they also do
not necessarily generate progress. In many cases, grating or eroding
relations of fit can realign in several directions. Technological inventions and developments, in particular, are notoriously ambivalent. The radio undoubtedly contributed to the emergence of a
democratic public sphere, but it was also the Nazis' most important tool in bending the masses to their will. Perhaps the Arab
Spring would never have occurred without mobile phones and social media, but the Islamic State also successfully exploited these
media for its anything but progressive ends.[65] Although new practices may be transformative, they are to a certain extent open-
ended. An invention can but does not have to bring about positive
social changes; and a social change can draw from several distinct
sources, such that constellations arise in which changes occur as
multiply overdetermined complexes of various dynamics of practice.[66] The Marxist optimism that the extraordinarily dynamic de-

velopment of the forces of production under capitalism, in creating untold misery, had also created the conditions for putting an end to that misery, thereby loses its empirical foundation. What is more, the criteria for determining the progressiveness of social transformation processes are also affected. Whereas the Marxist dialectic has an in-built true north, we are frequently dealing with multidimensional entanglements that lack compass points. So where can we find the normative lodestar for processes of social change? What makes them progressive—or not?

This chapter began with the question of how moral progress arises. I then shifted the terms of the question to examine the changes undergone by a whole complex of background conditions and follow-up practices in which moral attitudes and practices are embedded, as well as by the social interpretive horizon that gives them meaning. We found that moral progress is always based on *social* progress (broadly conceived), which involves more than just a correction to a society's moral ideas or normative principles. This redirected our attention to the fact that progress is a form of social change. In short: the question of moral change has transformed into the question of social change. In the next chapter, I will explore the formative conditions and dynamics of social change, before returning to the question of the normative lodestar in Chapter 5.

4

CRISIS AND CONFLICT

The Dynamics of Social Change

Revolutions require a *passive* element, a *material* basis. . . . It is not enough that thought strive to actualize itself; actuality must itself strive toward thought. —KARL MARX

Political revolutions are inaugurated by a growing sense . . . that existing institutions have ceased adequately to meet the problems posed by an environment that they have in part created.
—THOMAS KUHN

Things don't change if you don't force them to.
—VIRGINIE DESPENTES

PROGRESS IS CHANGE within change. To understand what progress is, we need to understand how social change works. If complex structures of practices or forms of life are the site of such change, as set out in the previous chapter, we must now move on to investigate how the transformational dynamic of such structures is constituted—how small- and large-scale changes in forms of life, social revolutions, and transformations present themselves to be recognizable as progressive.

As we have seen, social change becomes *possible* where there is a mismatch between different social practices and institutions, where relations of fit between them are disrupted, creating an entry point for change. But what is it that *motivates* social change? What drives or prompts it? This chapter proceeds from the assumption that the driving forces behind such transformations are problems, crises, and conflicts. New societies emerge from crises of the old order, to put it in Marxist terminology. Or with Hegel: societies are transformed when the contradictions that they themselves produce are sublated (at once cancelled, superseded, and preserved).

Although such crises are not solely brought about through the beliefs, intentions, and volitions of the actors concerned, actors are needed for them to turn into conflict. What role, then, do social actors play in the overall process? How should we picture the relationship between structural change—the gradual drifting and grinding of tectonic plates—and the moments when actors take matters into their own hands? Finally, how should we understand the "deflationary" logic of development promised in the Introduction? In this chapter, I am able to lay out not a comprehensive theory of social change, but only some of the key points for answering my initial question about progress. Accordingly, I first come back to the Marxist idea that any revolution or, more generally, social transformation process has a *passive* and an *active* element (4.1). I then turn to the dynamics of ways of life as problem-solving processes (4.2) to explain the sluggishness and blockages of transformation processes in terms of their integration in complex functional nexuses (4.3). This takes me to the question of crisis and conflict, and to the role played by actors and social movements in processes of social change (4.4). The chapter concludes with an exploration of what has emerged from my account as a labile or "fractured" logic of transformation, a logic that I contrast with the teleological idea of development (4.5).[1]

4.1 Active and passive elements

Revolutions, Marx writes, need "a *passive* element," a "*material* basis." It follows that they also need an active element. The key to understanding (progressive) change lies in understanding what these two elements are and how they relate to each other.

So, what exactly are the passive and active elements of revolution?[2] The difference seems obvious at first glance. The passive element are the social and material conditions that cry out to be changed or overthrown, as opposed to the active element, the committed revolutionaries who set out to change or overthrow them. Things appear less straightforward on closer inspection, however. What are these conditions if not the results of human action and volition, the products of social practice? And vice versa: what makes revolutionaries revolutionary? If revolutionaries (or the agents of social transformation) are those who seize the opportunities for change presented by conditions, the passive element, and if, conversely, these opportunities—the contradictions, crises, and dysfunctionalities of the prerevolutionary situation—are first brought to a head by the revolutionaries, does not the passive element produce the active and vice versa? Obviously, the two elements do not exist independently of each other: the occasion creates revolutionaries just as much as revolutionaries create the occasion. In what follows, I will first translate the idea of the active and passive element into the vocabulary of problems and contradictions, crises and conflicts, in order to interpret their interlocking on this basis.

Not from nowhere

With regard to the structure and dynamics of social change, the examples discussed in the last chapter already provide some clues as to what transformation processes might look like and how diversely the various dynamics interact. Under pressure from developments, innovations, or crises, elements become dislodged from a nexus of practices; traditional social practices lose importance (or even credibility) as they are joined by new social practices and techniques. This leads to all kinds of shifts. Some of these new practices can be assimilated into the existing ensemble. Others burst its bounds altogether, precipitating more or less far-reaching changes that can cause a form of life to change, or even disappear and be replaced.[3] Tried-and-tested relations of fit groan and buckle under the strain; they can and must be readjusted, the interpretive framework of practices reconfigured. New spaces, interstitial or otherwise, emerge as the architecture of the nexus is reorganized.[4] All this is accompanied by more or less explicit social debate about the process of readjustment and interpretation, of remaking, transforming, or even (in cases of doubt) preserving the social nexus of practices in which individuals lead their lives. And although I am dealing here with a nexus of practices, not some divinely ordained or naturally determined course of events, although we thus "make our own history," it also unfolds in some respects "behind our backs," as unintended consequences of our actions and as the effect of dynamics that lie beyond our grasp. It thus confronts us as an alien power. As should have become clear by now, social change (and even more: progressive social change) is therefore a confusing and messy affair.

For my purposes and for the theory of social change I can only sketch here, one aspect is crucial: social transformations do not come from nowhere. They react to a breakdown in existing practices and institutions when confronted with problems they can no longer solve or when beset by crises from which they cannot emerge without transforming themselves, and sometimes the entire frame of reference in which they stand. In a pragmatic spirit, it could therefore be claimed that social change is triggered by crises and upheavals; it reacts to the need to adapt to social situations that have become unclear—that is, to *problems*, *crises*, or even *contradictions* (in the strong Hegelian sense). These three different concepts all place emphasis on the reactive side: social change does not simply spring from a good idea, like Athena emerging fully grown from the head of Zeus, but is motivated by some form of dysfunctionality or obsolescence in the status quo. It arises in reaction to the fact that established practices have outlived their usefulness, that institutions have eroded or become riddled with contradictions. The question of how social change comes about does not then take the form: "Why does anything change at all?" In other words, it does not presuppose a static situation that would make it hard to see why anything should ever be different. Rather, social formations always present themselves as dynamic entities that are plagued by all manner of problems, lurch from one crisis to the next, and are pushed beyond themselves, so to speak, in certain situations and constellations. As a response to a challenge, the "new"—the novel social practice, institution, or formation and the new understanding of our practices—is a directed transformation within a constellation resulting from contradictions and grating relations of fit, or simply from signs of erosion in the "old order." Whether radical or not, social change is then a crisis-driven problem-solving process. This accounts for its dynamism as well as its directionality, which is what matters most when considering the question of progress.

A need for social change therefore arises whenever the erosion of social institutions and practices and the onset of new problems call for new practices and institutions. This is also what makes social change possible—although it alone does not make it real.[5] When new societies emerge from the crises of the old ones, social formations do not change just because a handful of actors (or even a majority) want them to, but because of the conditions those formations themselves have helped to create—conditions that allow, enable, suggest, and at times, it seems, almost compel the change. These are the situations in which the *ancien régime* totters on its foundations, or in which (to paraphrase Lenin) some no longer want to carry on in the old way and others no longer can.[6] As Hannah Arendt remarks, power then sometimes seems to be "lying in the street," which is not to say that it is always picked up.[7]

But what exactly does it mean to say that these developments are problem- or crisis-driven, or even that they follow a logic of "overcoming contradictions"? In the next section, I will pursue this question by again placing it in terms of the theory of practice introduced above, using this perspective to shed further light on the motif of problem-solving.

4.2 Forms of life as second-order problem-solving entities

Forms of life, understood as inert ensembles of social practices, are problem-solving entities. They embody reactions to problems, attempts to solve problems that arise *for* and *with* them. This is the premise for understanding their dynamics and the conditions under which they change. If forms of life are problem-solving entities in relation to always already normatively inflected and historically situated problems, then they change when confronted by new problems, signs of erosion, or crises in the social practices and institutions that they themselves have helped to create. In what follows, I will briefly unpack what it means to say that forms of life are problem-solving entities.

Problems as task and difficulty

What is a *problem*? My use of the term draws on a characteristic ambiguity. When we say that someone is faced with a problem, this can mean that they are confronted by either a task or a difficulty. Accordingly, referring to forms of life as problem-solving attempts can either mean that forms of coexistence are faced with certain *tasks* they have to solve (without it necessarily being implied that these tasks already pose difficulties), or it can mean that forms of life are confronted with *difficulties*, a situation in which something has become problematic or escalated into a full-blown crisis. A problem in this second sense appears where certain courses of action break down, interpretations go wrong, we find ourselves no longer doing what we want or wanting what we do, or something we thought we understood now baffles us. The use of the term proposed here sees both meanings as interwoven: forms of life always stumble upon problems in the sense of difficulties when coping with problems in the sense of tasks. Sometimes the (positive) task become visible only negatively, through the difficulties—or crises— that arise along the way. In both respects, forms of life are *reactive*, and in both respects, they react to material living conditions. They are thus in turn *shaped* by socially configured, normatively and historically inflected premises.

Problems, as I understand them in this context, are therefore culturally specific as well as historically and socially determined. They appear only in the context of a prefigured, determinate, historically situated, and socially instituted form of life, a situation already influenced by prior interpretations. Problems are thus not naked, "bare facts" that are simply lying in the street. Nonetheless, in a certain sense they escape our grasp, standing in our way and blocking us from performing actions.[8]

Problem-solving

To what extent do forms of life *solve* problems, and how do they do so? They solve problems by organizing our lives—that is, by placing at our disposal the patterns of action and institutions in which we live. In doing so, each form of life expresses its own particular problem status or problem level. Each represents a provisional attempt to address a certain problem-solving process that must be considered interminable. In understanding forms of life as problem-solving entities, we therefore begin *in media res*, in a world already shaped by practices and beset by problems. We are always already caught up in a problem-solving process.

For that reason, past problem-solving histories—a sequence of problems or crises and their (more or less successful) resolutions—are always sedimented in forms of life. Put differently: in going about their lives, people shape the material and immaterial (cultural and symbolic) conditions of those lives. The problems that repeatedly confront them are rarely solved once and for all. The more complex the situation, the less likely it is that problems can be solved without tension, since problem-solving typically brings forth new problems.

As an example, we can consider the theory of the family developed in Hegel's philosophy of right.[9] If that theory is to be believed, the bourgeois family transforms the traditional patriarchal family to actualize freedom in an institution in which attachment and independence are compatible, or in which the individual's instinctual needs can be sublimated and "fleeting desires" can be stabilized as an aspect of ethical life.[10] Yet as long as this family formation remains patriarchal—as long as it undermines the autonomy of its female members and posits a false dichotomy between nature and mind, between the particular and the general, between women's (supposedly) emotional nature and men's (supposedly) rational striving for universality—it comes under pressure and becomes mired in various crises. These are due not only to the potential for conflict built into this very family model but also to changes occurring in the world around it (for example, in the workplace). The redefinition of gender relations that takes place under these conditions and the opening of the family to non-heterosexual orientations and polyamorous experiments can be seen as reactions to this pressure and the ever more glaring shortcomings of the classic family model.

I speak of forms of life as problem-solving entities in order to ward off intentionalist misunderstandings. In saying that forms of life solve problems, I am not making them out to be subjects equipped with intentions and the capacity to act for themselves. As asserted above (in Chapter 3), it is instead a question of impersonal patterns of action and social structures that both provide and limit opportunities for individual actors. Still, human beings naturally play an active part in both the emergence and the decay of networks of social practices, if only because we are social actors who coproduce and reproduce such networks in going about our lives (although we may not "produce" them, as Marx would have it in claiming that human beings "produce their lives").

Second-order problems

The problems that impinge on forms of life *as* forms of life and in relation to which the question of progress can first be posed are typically *second-order problems.* This refers to problems concerning the conceptual and cultural resources that a form of life can draw on to tackle first-order problems. Take, for example, a predominantly agrarian society that is afflicted by famine after a prolonged drought. The lack of food is clearly a first-order problem for the reproduction of this society: people are starving to death. A *second-order problem* arises when for some reason the society proves incapable of taking appropriate measures to address this first-order problem. Second-order problems thus concern not the pressing food shortage but the social resources, practices, and institutions that make it possible (or impossible) to react to it. If periods of famine recur but the society fails to develop adequate responses— by building storage facilities, for example—then this inability to react is a second-order problem.

If climate change is already anthropogenic, then the roadblocks to learning and structural obstacles that stand in the way of a rational approach to the problem are a second-order problem. It may be that the society in question is overwhelmed by the sheer scale of the problem or denies its existence; it may not fully understand the natural processes involved, or it may even see starvation or climate change as sent by God. Such a second-order problem was evident in 2021, when the Governor of Utah called on people to pray for rain to replenish the Colorado River, which had dried up largely due to human activity.[11] Another example would be a society that has the wherewithal to solve a crisis—as is often the case with self-induced supply crises in the global economy—but lacks the (political) will to step up against certain economic and ecological dynamics. When second-order problems or crises become entrenched, this is always a sign that there is a problem with the form of life itself: that the established institutions, practices, beliefs, and commonplaces of that society have become debilitated and dysfunctional. They are faced with a blockage to learning.

As the possibilities I have just outlined for interpreting or denying a famine or climate change show, because perceptions of problems are themselves shaped by the normative expectations that both emanate from an institutional order and are directed at it, forms of life are confronted by crises on the basis of normatively predefined descriptions of the situation. The crises to which they succumb, and through which they can be driven beyond themselves to the brink of transformation, are therefore always also normative crises.

Progress as reflexive problem-solving

If forms of life are problem-solving entities in this sense, then they change precisely when confronted with new problems or crises that they have in part created, as Thomas Kuhn puts it, including signs of erosion in existing social practices and institutions. Problems in a social order—manifested in crisis symptoms and erosion phenomena—can have a variety of causes. Sometimes a social formation, threatened by external factors or rattled by new circumstances, technological developments, or other forms of social life, is plunged into a crisis that it lacks the material, social, or moral resources to overcome. Social practices and institutions can, however, also fray or erode due to inherent contradictions. Imagine, for example, a society that relied on caregivers and nurses but systematically undermined the supply of these essential services. Entire social orders can become dysfunctional and suffer a loss of legitimacy that may lead to spontaneous outbreaks of conflict.

The following point is key for the question of progress: progress or regression occurs when forms of life are confronted with second-order problems that they can either resolve (progress) or fail to resolve (regression). I said above that forms of life are inherently problem-driven, caught up in an ongoing problem-solving dynamic. What makes them *progressive* or otherwise, however, is not determined by whether they can solve the first-order problems that trigger this dynamic, but by whether they can solve second-order problems—that is, whether they have the institutional resources and levers needed for initiating reflexive problem-solving processes. The question is thus not whether they actually (sometimes or frequently) solve problems, or even whether they (sometimes or frequently) learn from these problems. The question is *whether they have learned to learn*. Social progress then primarily means progress in reflexivity with regard to problem-solving skills.

My account has a second consequence that helps us better understand progress. If the problems that need to be solved within a form of social life are heterogeneous—technical problems, problems of knowledge, problems of coexistence, political or social problems—then the interconnections and relations of fit between the various dimensions of progress can also be grasped at the level of second-order problem-solving capacities. Advances in technological problem solving, for example, will not betoken progress unless they take into consideration and prove commensurable with other dimensions of the social, their impact on these, and their possible side effects. Solutions to economic problems—the logic of maximizing utility—can stand in the way of solutions to social problems. At the level of second-order problems, however, these two aspects are not distinct. Progress in the development of production that benefits neither the individuals it consigns to the scrap heap of unemployment nor the environment it pollutes is unworthy of the name. Progress thus becomes a meta-category of social change; the question of whether a social change is progressive or regressive is decided not least by the integration of these very aspects.

Problem, crisis, contradiction

The picture that has emerged so far looks something like this: under normal conditions, forms of life are always changing simply because they are constantly forced to adapt to new situations. These are the run-of-the-mill problem-solving processes that make up the continuous dynamic of the social, and in which individuals participate in one way or another by rearticulating and reappropriating practices. In the course of this (normal) problem-solving process, however, forms of life sometimes end up in situations that call for more radical change. This is the case when the reference system within which problems are normally solved has itself become problematic. The problem-solving process is then in *crisis*, or as Alasdair MacIntyre would say, in an "epistemological crisis" that can initiate radical paradigm shifts. Crises are thus not quite the same as more pressing or somehow more daunting problems. They are an indication that the way in which problems are usually understood and addressed has stopped working. An increasingly dysfunctional situation is pushing toward a moment of decision.

The notion of contradiction has further-reaching, more demanding implications. Whereas a logical contradiction in the classical sense exists between two irreconcilable statements, socially induced *practical* contradictions arise when a set of social practices is constituted in such a way that it systematically undermines itself, making its continued functioning impossible. Contradictions are produced systematically and internally. They do not befall a social formation from outside and by chance, like a jogger falling victim to a mugging, but are built into the functioning of the formation itself. They are at once a condition of its functioning and its non-functioning, so to speak. As endemic problems generated by a given social formation, contradictions can therefore only be resolved through the (radical) transformation of that formation.

Crisis and conflict

What distinguishes crises, contradictions, and problems from *conflicts*? The first three have in common that they all refer to a type of *dysfunctionality*. A conflict, on the other hand, is an antagonism, a more or less violent disagreement between two or more parties. In this sense, crises and problems are "objective" (and hence a passive element) because they draw attention to a dysfunctionality or blockage on the side of things, while conflicts are "subjective" (and hence the active element) because they put such a situation up for decision within a field of possible courses of action and parties to the conflict. In this case, it is important to make clear that there is disagreement about *both* what constitutes a problem, a contradiction, or a crisis *and* about what it might take to resolve it. The resulting conflict spills over to the level of how the paradigm, the system of interpretation itself, is interpreted. To return to one of my examples, the Governor who called on the people of Utah to pray for rainfall would in all likelihood reject the idea that his state was suffering from a deficient problem-solving mechanism of the second order.

Starting out from the premise that forms of life are problem-solving entities, the pragmatist-materialist perspective I have adopted has suggested a fairly robust answer to the question of progress. If the dynamic of social change is understood as resulting from the contradictions, crises, and conflicts that traverse social formations, but also, less dramatically, from the simple tasks and problems they confront, then the progressiveness of a development can presumably be ascertained by determining whether it provides solutions to whichever problems have arisen. A development that solves the emergent problem could then be termed progressive. As we have seen, however, such an answer merely shifts the problem. Who decides what a problem is, and how do they decide it? What are the success criteria for a solution?

In many cases, as a glance at sociopolitical debates in recent years shows, there is considerable controversy over whether something should count as a problem, let alone a full-blown crisis. Was the so-called European refugee crisis in the summer of 2015 really a crisis—and if so, in what respect? Was the problem that people threatened by persecution in their homeland, or whose lives had otherwise been made intolerable, were now fleeing to Europe? Or was it rather that this gave far-right populist movements the pretext they needed to steer the social discourse in an authoritarian direction and spread fantasies of a "population exchange"? Clearly, even the terms in which the problem is cast are contentious—and the possible solutions all the more so.: Would the crisis be resolved if Europe were to seal off its borders in a bid to stem the tide of migrants, perhaps by building a big, beautiful wall? Or does the solution lie in granting refugees permanent asylum in the EU and giving them a political and social voice as fellow citizens? Not only are there differences of opinion here. There are also conflicts of interest that should not be underestimated. How crises or problems are perceived depends in part on *who* experiences a given situation as a crisis or problem. To take another example, if government-funded integration and social security services break down, this is surely disadvantageous or even catastrophic for those who depend on affordable public infrastructure, be it health insurance, unemployment benefits, or state-subsidized education. But why should this be a problem, let alone a comprehensive crisis of social integration, and not, say, a victory in the neoliberal crusade to liberate individuals to realize their full potential in an unfettered market economy? For some, high jobless figures represent a dramatic crisis of social integration, while for others, the growth of a "reserve army of labor" (Marx) or "production" of a precariat is a welcome opportunity to cut wage costs or further reduce minimum social standards. Crises are thus not only normatively constituted themselves (crises of normativity); calling something a crisis is also a normatively configured description that both reflects and informs a comprehensive evaluation of the situation.

4.3 Stability and instability of social formations

The description of social change ventured here is based on a premise that is anything but self-evident: that social formations and forms of life are intrinsically dynamic entities. Accordingly, social changes are always changes within a process of continuous change. Revolutionary and progressive action weaves in and out of these processes like a surfer catching a wave; sometimes it even steers them. Instead of asking how such apparently stable structures (to which individuals are bound for a variety of reasons) can be changed, we should ask *how the way they change can be changed.*

Change

Change, as the cliché has it, is the only constant. The transformation of our social world consists of countless more or less sweeping, more or less radical, more or less deliberate changes. Some occur without our active involvement or even against our will; others are the result of long-term planning or strategy. Some are limited to specific aspects of everyday life, while others affect the political or economic fabric of an entire society. Some are punctuated by a series of dramatic events (such as the fall of the Shah's regime in 1979 or the collapse of the GDR in 1989, closely followed by German reunification in 1990) or unfold with surprising rapidity (like the take-up of the PC and smartphone or the breakthrough of the #MeToo movement); others creep up on a society almost unawares (like the encroaching commercialization of the health system). Some are comprehensive and radical, such as the regime changes mentioned above or the "digital revolution," which has radically transformed society, the workplace, and the lifeworld. Others only concern micro-practices or certain areas of social life. On the other hand, these are often linked to more comprehensive changes, either because they are set off by such changes or because they can snow-ball into them. This can be seen in the seemingly harmless example of dietary change in the privileged countries of the global North, specifically Germany:

> Few areas of life have undergone such drastic changes in recent years as nutrition. Older generations can still remember a time when there were neither avocados nor papayas in this country, peanut butter was a rarity, and parsnips and parsley roots were not exactly common, either. In the late 60s, you could still meet people who had never eaten pasta. Today we can tell the difference between spaghetti, spa-ghettoni, and spaghettini.[12]

Decisions about what to buy, cook, and eat are micro-practices of everyday life. As we know, dietary habits do more than just ex-press economic status and local customs. They are also pervaded by social distinctions. If frozen food and fast-food restaurants were still a convenient option for dual-income families in the 1970s, by the 1990s they were sneered at as unwholesome fodder for the lower classes. Where parsnips were once confined to specialty shops, they can now be found in every local supermarket, while the once exotic avocado has not only become a domestic staple but has even been declared a superfood. Spaghetti, meanwhile, is probably Germany's favorite national dish. Despite their fast pace, changes of this kind are more than just fashion trends. They reflect broader social and economic changes: the globalization of trade, the internationalization of transport, the growing affluence of postwar Germany, and the social impacts of migration and tourism.

These apparently innocuous changes are always—at least in modern capitalist societies with a highly developed common infrastructure—also the result of economic processes and agricultural policies. There was nothing inevitable about the shift in meat consumption from a Sunday treat to standard (and inexpensive) everyday fare, which could never have happened without sustained political support for the meat and livestock sector.[13] While the changes described here express broader changes, they also trigger such changes. There is no doubt that consumer preferences in wealthy countries influence the global food situation and climate (as has been much discussed in the case of meat). This also applies to the health-conscious segments of the market, where the global boom in quinoa consumption, for example, has led to the degradation of agricultural land in parts of Peru.

Sluggish habits, stable social structures

Although social formations are inherently dynamic, they still contain elements that stand opposed to change. In Chapter 3, I described forms of social life as *inert* ensembles of practices. Practices may be made by human beings, but they do not stand entirely at our disposal. They condition and enable actions by providing a template for performing them. The performance of practices, as I have said, involves an element of habit—and habits have staying power. Social practices do not change as easily as opinions and beliefs. You don't join a form of life in the same way you do a football club. Whereas joining a club is as simple as filling out a form, you are socialized or acculturated into the dense network of conventions, priorities, and patterns of interpretation that constitute the associated form of life, without always knowing what you are doing. These patterns are also inscribed in the body and in bodily perceptions. Iris Marion Young's pioneering essay, "Throwing Like a Girl," vividly demonstrates how feminine role ascriptions determine spatial relations and physical mobility.[14] Breaking the hold of these fixed patterns can be difficult, and it is not by chance that emancipatory movements regularly start out by making such implicit patterns and inscriptions explicit.

The complexity of the ensemble structure also contributes to the inertia and thus stability of social structures or social networks (in the sense of a resistance to change). Every individual social practice is interwoven with many others; it needs them in order to exist and it refers to them. Complex social structures assign actors positions and behavioral norms within structures from which they cannot simply take their distance. If practices stabilize each other or even stand in a functional relationship to each other, it is impossible to break out of one practice without tearing down another. In some respects, then, a nexus of practice is firmly anchored and hard to dislodge, and this persistence has its counterpart in the emotional and sometimes ideological attachment it can inspire in individuals. Progressive or emancipatory social change can look like a process of sloughing off or unlearning irksome habits, sometimes through counter-practices.[15] But that is a misleading image, or at any rate an incomplete one. If the social world is in the grip of constant change, then we are also permanently changing our habits, precisely because the world in which we form them—the practical functional contexts in which they operate—is changing, too.

To come back to the example of diet: it is not just consumption habits (and certainly not individual preferences) that have led to the degradation of agricultural land in Peru but much broader economic settings. Expanding cultivation, not consumption, is causing Peru to dry out, driven not just by skyrocketing demand but by inadequate local regulation, profit interests, and/or a lack of commercially viable alternatives. The economically induced change that has fueled the boom in meat, avocado, and quinoa consumption becomes a second-order problem when it diverts attention from the ecological limits to this type of agriculture.

This prompts questions about second-order problems and the kind of blockages we are dealing with. Why do local and global societies seem incapable of solving the first-order problems that confront them (for example, drought caused by overexploitation)? Is a legal system that withholds rights from nature to blame? Or an economic system that allows costs to be externalized? Is capitalism the problem, with its logic of profit and growth? These are second-order problematizations (the question of the resources a society has for solving its problems) that admit a range of more or less far-reaching answers. The situation described here and the resources available represent the "passive element"—that is, the point from which people set out to thematize and change their living conditions: the concrete situation in which, all around the world, they must fight for their lives.

4.4 From crisis to conflict

Once we take the symptoms of crisis described above as the starting point for social change, the interlocking of the active and passive elements appears in a different light. If the erosion of the old order—the crisis (or series of crises) that befalls it—is the passive element, and if the active element is the fact that people are no longer willing to "play along" and resolve to take power into their own hands (or, in less heroic cases, relinquish or change their practices), then the two elements are interconnected to the extent that people's refusal to comply is precisely what makes conditions dysfunctional. And vice versa: people are no longer willing to play along because conditions are dysfunctional. The old order loses its legitimacy and social cohesion because it has stopped working, and it has stopped working because it has lost its legitimacy. Processes of factual change will then emerge along a continuum between the active and passive poles. Sometimes social actors react to the crisis; sometimes they precipitate it.

So far, the focus has been on the passive conditions for social change and the side of (objective) crises. It now shifts to the active moment. We have already seen that moral progress is not confined to changes in individuals' hearts and minds but encompasses transformations in social practice networks, social structures, or forms of life. The history of social progress additionally shows that progress is not usually achieved by well-meaning people changing their beliefs through learning processes and the polite exchange of arguments. In most cases, it has to be fought for by social movements. These struggles are more or less forceful, more or less radical, and more or less successful. They are often arduous, mounted in the face of massive resistance. Even hard-won victories have to endure the "travails of the plains" that, according to Brecht, follow on from the "travails of the mountains."[16] In certain historical moments—revolutions—events accelerate and condense. Other transformations unfold more tranquilly. Some social struggles are comprehensive or aim at sweeping changes; others deliberately address specific areas. It is not uncommon for there to be disputes among actors about which strategies and targets are best suited to achieving sufficiently far-reaching and therefore sufficiently radical change. In the words of Martin Luther King, the goal is "to create such a crisis and foster such a tension that a community which has constantly refused to negotiate is forced to confront the issue."[17] Put differently, if social change is premised on crises, then a precondition for it are processes capable of turning crises into conflicts.

The world-historical individual and the proletariat

Not the least merit of Marx's theory is to have conceptualized the relationship between active and passive elements in social change processes, up to and including revolutionary change. There is an unresolved tension in his work between the production of passive conditions for revolution, spelled out in a structural analysis within a materialistically reframed philosophy of history, and the class struggle in which these conditions are brought to a crisis and their transformation fought for by a self-consciously articulate collective subject. This tension can be traced in ever-changing historical constellations. We come across it in Hegel's reflections on the "world-historical individual" in his philosophy of history. Here, too, there is a tension between the world-historical individual's agency and the conditions under which that agency can be realized, or between the world-historical individual as heroic subject and its description as someone who merely realizes what is "timely":

> These are the great men in history, whose own particular purposes comprehend the substantial content which is the will of the world spirit. . . .
> Such individuals had no consciousness of the idea as such in pursuing their ends; on the contrary, they were practical, political men. But they were at the same time thinking men, who had an insight into what was necessary and timely. And this is the truth of their time and their world, as it were, the next race that was already internally present. Their affair was to know the universal, the necessary next phase of their world, turn it into their purpose, and put all their energy into it. World-historical individuals, the heroes of an age, must therefore be recognized for their percipience; their words and deeds are the best things of their age.[18]

For the historical process described by Hegel, world-historical individuals play an ambivalent role comparable to that ascribed to the proletariat by Marx. As managers of the world spirit, so to speak, they are genuine change-makers and revolutionaries who work to overcome the old state of affairs and impose new conditions. In so doing, however, they merely act on behalf of the world spirit, the historical situation expressing the "truth of their time and their world." They act because they have "an insight into what was necessary and timely" that guides them as they bring to light "what was already internally present." World-historical individuals thus react both actively and passively; they make history precisely by realizing its latent tendencies and possibilities. What happens historically depends on the contingent appearance of individuals or on the militant determination of the proletariat, transformed from a "class-in-itself" into a "class-for-itself." At the same time, however, it obviously depends no less on the historical situation, the world-historical conjunction—not just fortuitously arising possibilities (a sudden power vacuum sparking a revolt, for example) but systematic tensions and signs of debility in the existing social and institutional order. As Marx famously put it: "Men make their own history, but they do not make it just as they please; they do not make it under circumstances chosen by themselves, but under circumstances directly encountered, given and transmitted from the past."[19]

This tension between world-historical freedom and determinism can be defused if events are interpreted as realizing latent opportunities and possibilities. To be sure, such possibilities can remain unrealized if the constellation is inauspicious, or if there are no world-historical individuals at hand to seize the initiative. The realization of a potential built up over the course of history may be rational in the light of its prehistory and accompanying conditions, but it is never inevitable. The world-historical individual or relevant political subject is the one who turns up at the right time at the right place to do the right thing, acting upon the tendencies of the time to channel them into a viable future. Only in retrospect does this intervention seem inevitable.

We are now in a position to qualify what it means for (radical) social change to be possible. A range of resources and plethora of possibilities lend themselves to whichever "determinate" answer is chosen at any given historical moment. Just as social contradictions are first manifested as crises and "realized" as contradictions when they erupt into conflict, the latent resources and potentials for overcoming and renewing a form of life that has eroded or become obsolete only reveal themselves as such at the moment of crisis-induced transformation. We see this where a form of life that has entered a critical condition is subjected to sustained assault by social groups, such as feminists in the case of rape and rebelling slaves and abolitionists in the case of slavery.[20] Here, the erosion of social practices and institutions is not passively endured but actively aided and abetted by those seeking to overthrow them.

From the perspective adopted here, we could say that social conflicts and struggles contribute to changing the aggregate state of latent crises or signs of erosion. Accordingly, a criterion emerges for distinguishing not only between appropriate and inappropriate problem-solving but also between appropriate and inappropriate (or: progressive and regressive) social struggles. Changes that react appropriately to problems and crises are progressive, whereas those that perpetuate or produce blockages to experience and learning are regressive. I will pursue this idea further in Chapter 5, which will ask how social changes can be evaluated as progressive. My account of social change as a problem-solving process nonetheless allows some initial conclusions to be drawn regarding the question of developmental logic.

4.5 Roads not taken: Developmental logics and experiential processes

Social change does not come from nowhere, I claimed earlier. It is provoked by upheavals of all kinds. But how does it occur? What (additional) logic dictates its development? To quote Trotsky's reflections on the Russian Revolution: "Events can neither be regarded as a series of adventures, nor strung on the thread of a preconceived moral. They must obey their own laws."[21] But what are those laws, and how strictly do they operate? How can a logic supposedly governing enrichment, learning, and the accumulation of experience be made plausible? And what distinguishes it from the kind of developmental logic I problematized in my introduction? My thesis is that the new (the novel social practice, institution, or formation and the new understanding of these practices) is the result of a directed transformation within a constellation that emerges from the contradictions, disrupted relations of fit, and/or signs of erosion of the "old order." Whereas the extraordinarily ambitious orthodox version of this thesis, which is oriented on the logic of practical contradictions, assumes that the new gestates within the old, such that the contradiction already contains within it the seeds of its own resolution, the connection can also be understood more loosely: as a constitutively open-ended experiential and problem-solving process.

I claimed earlier that reactions to problems are instantiated in forms of life. These also bear within them sedimented *problem-solving histories*, a palimpsest of past problems or crises with their (more or less successful) resolutions, from which the next set of problems then arises. One problem solution builds on the next. We are thus dealing here with conditions that have taken on their present form because they emerged from what came before and reacted to its specific shortcomings in a relationship of succession or divergence. Social experiences—the erosion and transformation of existing social practices and institutions—follow on from each other in a way that is either constructive, in the sense that it allows for enriched learning and a qualitative deepening of experience, or destructive, in the sense that it blocks adequate opportunities for experience and prevents learning. This assumption of cumulative enrichment or impoverishment clearly suggests that social experiences react to each other or proceed from each other. It does *not* imply, however, that such a process must have a definitive end or goal, or that it unfolds teleologically, with the germ of the unfolding process already contained in the starting point of the development. Predefined developmental stages thus have no place in the model sketched here.

This is due not least to the fact that problem-solving processes do not always successively tackle one and the same problem. They do not work incessantly on a specific cluster of *fundamental and timeless* anthropological conundrums that would be solved only at the end of history, if at all. Problem-solving is a free-standing process that cannot be understood in teleological terms as the realization of a goal inherent to human life. Just as meaning only arises in the process of meaning-making, the problems we are concerned with here only arise *in actu* and within a complex dynamic. As in a game of whack-a-mole, they keep popping up in different locations, summoned partly by previous problem solutions and partly by the new practical tasks and challenges that rise to meet us. In the process, not only the means for solving problems undergo successive transformations but also the ends.[22]

Problem-solving is thus an ongoing, dynamic process, an open-ended experiential or learning journey. A problem is not solved once and for all, nor does it recur in the same form while inviting new possible solutions each time. Instead, problems change with and over the courses of their solutions. It is not only the solutions that are always new but the problems themselves, not just because new demands are constantly being placed on given social formations but also because these formations develop immanently, engendering problems at ever higher—mediated—levels.

Because problems always result from prior solutions and entail additional problems, and because human action and ingenuity are essential to the problem-solving process, solutions cannot be predicted in their entirety. Problems do not come with ready-made solutions. And even though crises may be impelled by an immanent logic—the logic of practical contradictions—they still react to unforeseeable circumstances and conditions, so an element of contingency is in play. Regression and progress—more precisely, the lines of development in relation to which we can differentiate between regressive and progressive trajectories—are thus *contingent but not arbitrary.* They follow a logic of possibilities that build on each other and presuppose each other without necessarily having to be realized.

A weak, multidimensional logic of history

A hurricane or drought can bring about the downfall of a government or spark a revolution, just as rich oil reserves can prop up an oppressive regime. And sometimes chance historical events can trigger processes that shake a system to its foundations. The opening of the Berlin Wall in November 1989 was famously set in motion by Günther Schabowski's impromptu announcement that travel restrictions for East Germans would be lifted "immediately, without delay," prompting citizens to stream uncontrolled—and now uncontrollably—across the border to West Berlin.[23] Nonetheless, it would be wrong to claim that this and subsequent events would never have happened if Schabowski had chosen his words more carefully. For all that he may have cut the figure of a bumbling bureaucrat, in that historical moment he was the Hegelian "world-historical individual," the actor who realizes and articulates the spirit of the age by bringing forth something new.

Even if sudden and contingent windows of opportunity can precipitate events, anyone who has lived through such processes of radical and accelerated social change on a large or small scale knows that a range of factors typically come into effect here: *longer-term* (economic problems, great-power rivalry, political reforms in the Gorbachev era), *medium-term* (pressure from mass emigration and the Monday demonstrations held in Leipzig and elsewhere), and very *short-term* (the irreversibility of the situation after Schabowski's announcement, which came about because people took his words literally and were unwilling to wait for the wheels of bureaucracy to grind into motion). These different factors can each claim a stronger or weaker internal logic and interact in a variety of ways. The fact that power is sometimes lying in the street and can be picked up does not mean that this is possible at any given moment.

Germany thus did not owe its so-called reunification to a slip of the tongue, nor were events fated to transpire exactly as they did. There are preconditions for certain possibilities arising in the first place, but there is nothing inevitable about any particular possibility becoming reality. There are "roads not taken" leading to other potential outcomes. The junctions in world history at which a different solution might have come about—in this case, alternatives to the accession of the eastern states to the Federal Republic of Germany, such as a new national constitution or an independent German state with its own economic and social order (as some of the groups involved in the revolution had initially envisaged)—can be hard to discern. The mere fact, however, that such alternatives have almost completely faded from memory shows how successfully the path taken in the end has suppressed all other possibilities.

So, things could always have turned out differently, even if the actual course of events is anything but arbitrary. A basis is needed for historical constellations to move in a particular direction and disclose certain possibilities for action, but there is more than one set of sufficient conditions for bringing this about. If, as I have suggested, we assume the existence of functional equivalents in the problem-solving process, then new paths will branch out, new problem threads and their solutions will unspool, depending on which equivalent is chosen.

Among multiple diverging options, the road that is eventually taken on the basis of the route set by one of these functional equivalents will progress with its own logic, according to the rationality of its own problems, and hence in the form of its own "rational response" to those problems.[24] "Roads not taken" are not simply there as roads.[25] They are at some point possible but, "knowing how way leads on to way," they disappear once a particular path has been chosen. Their not having been taken consigns them to nonexistence. Unlike real forks in the road, there is no path until it is chosen. It comes into being as it is traveled—or it never does.

5

CHANGE FOR THE BETTER?

Progress as a Self-Enriching Learning Process

The path must arise as you walk it. —KIM DE L'HORIZON

Everyone thinks that what comes out at the end of a bildungsroman is some kind of inevitable consequence of human existence. But all it does is reflect a writer's obsessional neurosis. Goethe's OCD. His need to line up his erasers parallel to the edge of his desk is the reason we all believe that we emerge from the chaotic jungle of painful experiences smarter than when we fell in.

—HELENE HEGEMANN

NOT EVERY CHANGE is for the better. Not every change denotes progress. In this chapter, I will turn to the question of which processes of social transformation can be understood as progressive—that is, to the distinction between progressive and regressive change. This brings me to the actual bone of contention, so far as the problem of progress is concerned, and to my central thesis that progress can be defined in processual rather than substantive terms, as a form of social change that itself acquires normative significance. Progress is then not only, as the formulation discussed in Chapter 1 would have it, a change for the better. It is a self-enriching experiential learning process.

To flesh out this thesis, I will first, inspired by a discussion in Robert Musil's novel *The Man Without Qualities*, provide a systematic account of what exactly makes defining progress so difficult. Progress "in a determinate sense," as Musil writes, can easily be ascertained.[1] But we always run into difficulties when it comes to identifying a sense that transcends such local advances (5.1). The approach developed below regards the question of whether there can be progress in this global sense as one that not only cannot be answered but cannot even be meaningfully posed. Societies do not pursue goals: they solve problems. Spelling out this assumption allows us to arrive at a non-teleological, pragmatist model of progress as a process of "growth" or enrichment (5.2). I then explore the negativist character of this process. The crucial criterion for evaluating progress, in my view, is that there are no blockages to learning and experience. Put differently: progress is the absence of regression (5.3).[2] In an excursus at the end of the chapter, I discuss the dialectical nature of the enrichment processes asserted here using the example of two emancipatory processes (5.4).

5.1 Part of the problem: Determinate and overarching senses of progress

Robert Musil's *The Man Without Qualities* is in some respects a novel about progress and its ambivalences. Set in the period immediately before the First World War, it repeatedly foregrounds changes in society and the lifeworld, as well as the epochal mood of a crisis of meaning in the bourgeois world. In one characteristic scene, Ulrich, the novel's protagonist, reminds his dinner companions that their assumptions about progress are not as self-evident as they think:

> But Ulrich was enjoying himself. "Is the modern house, with its six rooms, maid's bath, vacuum cleaner, and all that, progress, compared with the old houses with their high ceilings, thick walls, and handsome archways, or not?"
> "No!" Hans Sepp shouted.

"Is the airplane progress, compared with the stagecoach?"

"Yes!" Director Fischel shouted.

"The machine compared with handicrafts?"

"Handicrafts!" from Hans, and "Machine!" from Leo.

"It seems to me," Ulrich said, "that every step forward is also a step back. Progress always exists only in a determinate sense."[3]

Setting the superior comforts of modern homes against the absence of "thick walls and handsome archways," the exchange neatly illustrates the potential for fundamental differences of opinion on what counts as progress and the ambivalence of progress itself.

The ambivalence of progress

We could question the generalizability of Ulrich's insight that "every step forward is also a step back" in view of the abolition of slavery or the criminalization of domestic violence. Still, his reference to the different respects in which something presents itself as progress, to the "determinate" or determinable "sense" in which something is progressive, is illuminating. The railroad is a step forward in terms of speed, though perhaps not with regard to the sensory experience of travel or its effects on the environment. As we know, this was already the subject of heated debate at the time the railroad was invented.[4] With regard to comfort, modern housing is a step forward, but not necessarily in terms of its aesthetic appeal. When households switch to washing their clothes in washing machines, the form of sociality captured in nostalgic images of "washerwomen by the river" is lost.[5] Since the dawn of the Industrial Revolution, controversy has raged over the alienating tendencies of machine work compared to manual labor, and hence over whether there is anything inherently progressive about increased productivity. To illustrate the problem of ambivalence with an example less fraught with cultural pessimism, consider the introduction of diversity measures at universities. In some respects, this new way of quantifying academic performance promotes a progressive, emancipatory agenda of inclusion while simultaneously enforcing a standardized mainstream. And the (progressive) dismantling of organizational hierarchies sometimes goes hand in hand with a neoliberal culture of ruthlessly competitive careerism. Even in relation to relatively uncontentious moments of social progress, then, losses and ambivalences can often be weighed up against the gains.

And yet, insofar as the advances and setbacks described here relate to different aspects, it would be misleading to conclude with Ulrich that "every step forward is also a step back." The accelerated mobility of the airplane or train compared with the stagecoach is not a backward step in terms of mobility itself. It is one solely in terms of its side effects or performance on dimensions other than speed. In this sense, every change is accompanied by side effects—sometimes unexpected or unforeseeable—that can be negative, or even fatal, without for that reason discrediting the change itself. To obtain an appropriately complex picture, we need to pick apart and spell out the different ways in which something can be a step forward on the one hand and a step back on the other. The former in one respect may go hand in hand with the latter in another, but this does not condemn the criterion of progress to obsolescence, nor does it make progress generally ambivalent.

To be sure, criteria are needed to differentiate between the various respects and weigh them up against each other. Narrow medieval laneways may have their charm, yet no one would find them charming enough to put up with the diseases that thrive in damp, crowded, unsanitary conditions. The mass production of some consumer goods may come at the cost of diminished quality, yet the ability to supply everyone with them could be seen as preferable to the exclusiveness of artisanal production. Some things will remain ambivalent in Ulrich's sense. But once we pick apart the different aspects, we will find that in many cases the backward steps or

problematic side effects are not irrevocably bound up with progress. If we wanted to keep both the washing machine and a spirit of
neighborliness, appliances could be socialized by setting up communal laundries; or we could use the time saved by no longer
having to hand-wash clothes for other communicative purposes.
Even if diversity policy in its now-dominant form was first made
possible by the neoliberalization of the university—an administra-
tive regime that pits academic workers against each other in an
unending round of application procedures and evaluations—it is
not diversity policy that has produced the neoliberal university.[6]
Ulrich's claim that every step forward is also a step back is thus
untrue if we take it to mean that every change represents a step
forward and a step back *in the same respect.*

Progress in a determinate sense

Still, Ulrich's conclusion that there is no such thing as progress as
such, only progress "in a determinate sense," seems unobjectionable at first. Why should the invention of the airplane be an advance over the stagecoach? It is so only "in a determinate sense," to
the extent that it expedites the transportation of people and goods.
The modern home with its vacuum cleaner and washing machine is
a step forward because it takes less time and effort to clean. A factory machine is an advance over manual labor insofar as it allows
larger quantities to be produced with greater efficiency. That "progress always exists only in a determinate sense," as Ulrich says, thus
clearly means that progress is only ever recognizable within an existing means-end relationship and in relation to a predetermined
goal or purpose. The development of the microchip is a step forward only if our goal is to optimize computing power; the invention
of the vacuum cleaner or washing machine is a gain only if our goal
is to reduce time spent on housework. Antibiotics are an advance
because we want to fight infectious diseases. These inventions are

suitable means for realizing the purposes we uphold. In the unlikely event that we decide no longer to value and seek to optimize health, speed, or comfort, the developments mentioned above would stop being progressive.

The fact that we find it so easy to identify progress in these examples—for all their possible ambivalences and unintended side effects—is not because they concern basic areas of life or involve technological advances. It is because the *determinate sense* and purpose in relation to which they are progressive is so blatantly obvious. It is thus uncontroversial to label them such.

Things seem different when it comes to social and moral progress. These are controversial in every respect. Yet here, too, identifying instances of social or moral progress would be relatively straightforward if only it were possible to define goals, and hence a framework for evaluating individual developments as progressive. If we set the greatest possible prosperity as the goal of social coexistence, then the progress made by a social order can be gauged by its success in promoting prosperity. If the goal is to secure an evenly distributed, high-quality standard of living by providing the global populace with food, education, and opportunities to get ahead in life, then criteria could be developed for measuring progress toward this goal, even if they would have to be more complicated than mere GNP.[7] If diversity, inclusion, or an end to discrimination is the top priority, then the introduction of quotas or affirmative action programs undertaken with this aim in mind are progressive. If our goal is to reduce domination and violence in all spheres of social life, then the elimination of "*all conditions* in which man is a debased, enslaved, neglected, contemptible being," however complex, varied, and radical the changes required may be, is a step in the right direction.[8] Social progress is no different than technological progress, even if the choice of means for achieving the desired end may be incomparably more difficult and controversial: as soon as we can identify a goal, progress toward it can also be measured.

Here, too, progress is always progress in a determinate sense, and so long as advances can be related to that sense, evaluating a change as progressive seems almost trivial.

Progress as a whole

Far from trivial, and indeed in most cases hotly disputed, is the question of how such a goal ought to be defined. As *The Man Without Qualities* indicates, whenever it is no longer just a matter of effectiveness but of the impact of technological developments on the forms of life they influence, consensus often breaks down. It is relatively easy to agree that washing machines make for easier housework, computers for more efficient data processing, and trains for quicker journeys.[9] It is much harder to agree upon the no longer "determinate" or limited sense in which it is progressive to make data processing more effective, housework more convenient, information more accessible, travel faster, work more productive, and domestic life more comfortable. This is precisely what Ulrich means when he contends that "progress always exists only in a determinate sense": for him, the overarching progress in relation to which this determinate sense could be determined and classified is indeterminable.

The "man without qualities" here finds himself on the same page as a number of contemporary authors. He thus touches on one variant from the broad spectrum of positions that might be termed relativist (though we could also avoid this term, given the occasionally polemical tenor of the debate). According to these authors, there is progress in relation to this or that problem and always only within a determinate, set (practical and normative) context, not in an overarching or global, context-transcending sense.[10] In other words, there are local or sectoral progresses (in the plural) but there is no universal progress (in the singular). As Ulrich himself goes on to emphasize during the discussion in Diotima's salon: "Progress always exists only in a determinate sense. And since there is no sense in our life as a whole, neither is there such a thing as progress as a whole."[11]

Relativizing the purchase of the criterion of progress in this way sounds promising and plausible, especially as it addresses an undeniable source of embarrassment: it makes allowances for the immense historical and local, synchronous and diachronous plurality of social and ethical contexts. This makes it difficult to define the framework needed for an overarching definition of progress that transcends local (and hence determinate) contexts. In light of the diversity of possible normative orientations and established traditions, any agreement that escapes the charge of ethnocentrism and false, ideological-parochial universalization will be hard to reach. Not just in philosophy but in "real life," too, there is profound disagreement about which goals we should prioritize over others and how we should be able to do so without remaining tied to a particular position.[12]

At second glance, however, this "deflationary" solution, achieved by abandoning the grand canvas of Progress for the more modest miniatures of local progresses, turns out to be all too limited and in some respects trivial. Determinate or local progress is only such in relation to a set but not further justifiable goal, and this goal can only be considered progressive within an in turn determinate and thus limited frame of reference or context, which is itself accepted as unquestionably given.[13]

Does not the definition of progress "in a determinate sense," as Ulrich presents it in *The Man Without Qualities*, itself rely on a framework linking these determinate, local progresses to a higher goal if the changes in question are to count as progressive in any meaningful sense? We find ourselves caught in an infinite regress that can only be brought to a halt decisionistically. Rorty, for one, embeds his definition of progress in an avowed commitment to the social-liberal world order, making clear that this is precisely what is required: a *commitment*.

The problem is that hailing something as progressive in this way ultimately becomes trivial or tautological. It is progressive because we have learned in a determinate and therefore particular context to see it as such. The emancipation of slaves, workers, women, queers, and so on would then be progressive only within a particular framework. In short: progress is whatever we take it to be. While the deflationary strategy of confining progress to local or sectoral progresses is not directly refuted by this, its usefulness becomes moot. We need only recall the recent uprising of Iranian women—the "Woman, Life, Freedom" movement—and other virulent contemporary conflicts to see the need for a more robust and meaningful position. In this respect, the deflationary position is both philosophically and politically limiting. Philosophically, it quickly takes us to a place where no further justifications can be given, the "bedrock" where, in Wittgenstein's words, "my spade is turned."[14] Politically, it not only leaves us toothless, but also deprives us of the ability to provide explanation and critical analysis, precisely because it has nothing to say about the genesis of norms and wants nothing to say about the validity of the context itself, the evaluative framework within which something can normatively count as progress.

Should we then simply reverse Ulrich's conclusion? Can there be any progress in a local sense without progress "as a whole," in a global sense that transcends context? Where would the sense of direction come from if the sense of the sense must remain undetermined? I am tempted to say that if progress "as a whole" cannot be determined, then neither can progress "in a determinate sense." The sense of the sense—the respect in which the "determinate sense" of individual progressive developments makes sense within an overarching context—could then not be bracketed out when we come to evaluate those individual developments, precisely because a context always refers to the next, larger framework. If there is progress only in a determinate (set, locally restricted) sense, then the determining factor, the source from which the determinate meaning is determined, is assumed to be unquestionably given. But if the merely local evaluation of progress takes as self-evident the evaluative framework itself, it remains parasitically dependent on this normative framework and the criteria for evaluation set with it. To stay with the examples mentioned above: efficiency as a yardstick for the sense of technological advances would be no less fixed than the ideas of wellbeing, freedom, autonomy, or equality, insofar as these provide the framework for social and moral progress. These would then present themselves as simply "facts of life."[15] They would correspond to the understanding that "we"—a certain epoch, society, community of values, or tradition—have of ourselves, and which we cannot retreat from without harm to that self-understanding. In my opinion, this approach is inadequate, not least because it always implies a homogeneous "we" that strikes me as implausible in view of the real social conflicts.

We would then be facing a problem. On the one hand, a substantive, higher goal of progress (let alone of human development) cannot readily be determined; on the other, without such a goal we cannot even speak of local or sectoral progress in anything other than a redundant or trivial and parasitical way.

5.2 Part of the solution: progress as mode of enactment

Yet perhaps here, as so often, the question is framed incorrectly and we are confronted with a false alternative. Perhaps the question of the "sense as a whole" not only cannot be answered but is not even meaningfully posed. From the fact that local progresses—progress in a determinate and hence substantive sense—can be determined, Ulrich (and others) evidently conclude that "progress as a whole," progress in an overarching, global sense, would likewise have to be determined substantively. And if this should prove impossible—

and I have already set out the difficulties involved—then the only remaining option is to take flight into relativism, to accept that it cannot be determined *at all*. The way out of the dead end I propose is this: the "overarching sense" cannot be thought and evaluated in *substantive* terms—that is, in terms of *content*—but only as a *process* and in relation to its *form*.

To clarify this idea, let us return once again to Ulrich's comments: "Progress always exists only in a determinate sense. And since there is no sense in our life as a whole, neither is there such a thing as progress as a whole." Detecting "progress as a whole" accordingly depends on having access to a sense of "life as a whole." But what would it mean for "life as a whole" to have a sense? If there was a "sense in our life as a whole," as I understand Ulrich's reference to "sense," then it would have to be oriented toward something, toward a determinate and definable goal. Life would then have a sub-ject matter—namely, the attainment of this goal—and progress would be determinable from this goal, as its step-by-step realiza-tion. Ulrich is quite right to argue that "life as a whole" has no such goal, at either an individual or a societal level. We can see now why the alternative posed above is false: the framework we are looking for, the sense capable of giving individual changes a higher meaning, is not missing by chance, nor could it be found if only we were to search for it long enough. Its absence is necessary.

It may be instructive at this point to elucidate the position out-lined here with an insight from Sigmund Freud. Freud also assumes that the question of the meaning of life is not only factually un-solved but in principle insoluble. He writes: "The question of the purpose of human life has been raised countless times; it has never yet received a satisfactory answer and perhaps does not admit of one."[16] Why does it not admit of one? In effect, we are dealing here with a category mistake. Having "been raised countless times," the question of the meaning of life suggests that it can be determined impartially, as something that lies outside our lives and guides how we conduct them. According to Freud, this attitude is misguided. Indeed, merely asking the question indicates a problem, or even a pathology: "The moment a man questions the meaning and value of life, he is sick, since neither has any existence in an objective sense."[17] Anyone who questions the meaning of life in this way is "sick" because they adhere to a reified and falsely objectifying notion of the meaning of life. Life makes sense only from within, from how we go about our lives, and in a way that causes the question itself to dissolve. As soon as we ask about the meaning of life, it has disappeared; raising the question is already a symptom of unhappiness and depression.

While I cannot pursue this argument any further here, Freud's reflections inspire me to question the image that might hold us captive with respect to progress. Just as the question of the meaning of life is problematic—and ultimately lacks an object—from Freud's perspective, the idea of determining an overarching sense in the life of human societies, which could then become the benchmark for a likewise overarching progress, may lack an object too. This would not necessarily be bad news, not just because of the prevailing disagreement about what such a goal might be in the first place, but also because the idea of an overarching sense tempts us to reduce individual instances of social life to mere means toward an end that is clearly determined (howsoever and by whomsoever that may be) and therefore apparently objectively fixed, but above all imposed from without. Such an idea would be intrinsically wrong. One can learn vocabulary with the aim of mastering a foreign language, or enroll in goalkeeper training with the aim of conceding fewer goals in a soccer match. But personal and social life cannot become a means to an end in the same way. It is always already the game itself.

My thesis is therefore: just as "there is no sense in our life as a whole," societies as such have no goal. They solve problems. Determining a substantive overarching goal of social progress is not only impracticable, but also unnecessary. If forms of life are to be understood as problem-solving entities, as we saw in Chapter 4, then this primarily denotes a movement *away from*, not *toward*, as described in Chapter 1.[18] This movement is motivated and driven by problems that come to light as the practices constituting a form of life are performed and as the institutions that sustain it are maintained and expanded.

This view also provides a solution to the problem discussed above. The criteria for progressive or regressive dynamics do not arise from the substantive determination of progress toward a goal. They emerge in the process itself, from the progressive or regressive mode in which the changes in question are enacted.

Doing away with the old meaning

How then do we recognize whether a change is enacted appropriately—whether it is progressive or regressive? This is where the moment of enrichment comes into play, which I will examine more closely in the next section. In preparation, it may be useful to consider another argument that Musil puts in the mouth of his "man without qualities":

> Ulrich had paralyzed their tongues, but his fighting spirit was undiminished. He went on evenly: "But you can also say the opposite: If our life makes progress in the particular instance, it also makes sense in the particular instance. But once it has made sense to offer up human sacrifice to the gods, say, or burn witches, or powder your hair, then that remains a meaningful attitude to life, even when more hygienic habits and more humane customs represent progress. The trouble is that progress always wants to do away with the old meaning."[19]

Ulrich's assertion that the trouble with the previous understanding of progress (as an understanding that leads to the insolubility of the problem of progress) was that it "always want[ed] to do away with the old meaning," aiming to replace the meaning of an old age with the meaning of a new one, suggests at first a position of historicist relativism. The meaning but also legitimacy of a social practice could accordingly only be understood and gauged from its time and in its context. If the historical fashion of "powder[ing] your hair" made sense at that time and in that context, then its sense cannot be "do[ne] away with" from the position of later practices. If we accept Ulrich's reasoning, practices cannot be criticized from an external standpoint, one that transcends the context of their enactment, because they are only understandable and indeed justifiable in relation to this specific context.

That may not matter to us when it comes to powdered hair. Irritatingly, however, Ulrich includes (so-called) witch-burning and human sacrifice among the past practices associated with a "meaningful attitude to life."[20] His thesis might therefore be described as a crude moral relativism. There is a difference, however, between *understanding* a social practice or social order from its sociohistorical context and *justifying* it with reference to this context. Just because something is a "meaningful attitude to life" does not make it normatively appropriate.

I therefore do not interpret Ulrich's comments as moral relativism. In my view, his plea not always to "do away with the old meaning" is above all an attack on linear and normativist conceptions of progress. I take it to mean that if progress should not simply "do away" with the old life, the old customs and conditions, "the old meaning," then this is neither because the old still holds its own against the new, nor because this meaning withdraws relativistically from any evaluation applied to it from outside the given context. Instead, the "old meaning" is not to be "do[ne] away with" because the superseded way of life is not a mere mistake or normative error that could be refuted and dismissed. From the perspective of progress, the old life, the old ways, the old meaning are not just plain wrong. Powdered hair does not become wrong (for the period when it was fashionable) because we now consider it unhygienic and aesthetically outmoded. Aesthetically speaking, it cannot be wrong anyway, at most *passé*; and as a practice of personal hygiene, it cannot have been wrong back then. It was simply a convenient means of combating body odor and absorbing excess grease, albeit one that has since made way for different practices.

This assessment, however, is not straightforwardly applicable to the other examples of witch-burning and human sacrifice. What is wrong and inappropriate in these cases has nothing to do with aesthetic preferences or practices made obsolete by the onward march of technoscientific innovation or everyday routines. But even witch-burning and human sacrifice, I would argue, cannot simply be done away with by branding them "wrong." There is no doubt that these practices *are* wrong, no less than that they are cruel. But they are more than that. Moral condemnation alone misunderstands the nature of the inappropriateness of these practices. In this respect, a premature or blanket (decontextualized) normative judgment obscures the phenomenon. More precisely, it prevents us from understanding the conditions for normatively evaluating the problem and hence for analyzing, critiquing, and solving it.

The caution Ulrich calls for in relation to the "old meaning" does not have to mean that everything made sense in its day and is therefore exempt from judgment. Quite the contrary: precisely because it once made sense, it can be criticized on the basis of that specific meaning. Context-sensitive understanding and analysis are practically a prerequisite for incisive critique. It is not the case, as the French saying would have it, that to understand all is to forgive (or justify) all. The brutal example of so-called witch-burning clearly illustrates this: sociohistorical and genealogical studies such as Silvia Federici's *Caliban and the Witch* have demonstrated the social relevance and underlying political significance of persecuting wise women, along with the many and far-reaching social consequences that came from eradicating repositories of female knowl-

edge and practice.[21] Understanding the "sense" and context of
witch-burning then means no longer seeing it merely as the effect of
superstition, at once cruel and ridiculous in its cruelty, within a
medieval social order already marked by breathtaking cruelty; it
means understanding the (ideological) rationality and function
bound up with this practice—and thereby being able to criticize it
in a way that goes beyond self-satisfied censure.[22] Whereas "do[ing]
away with the old meaning" can involve taking the moral high
ground to deplore and denounce a bygone practice fundamentally,
yet in some respects inconsequentially, the critical analysis I have in
mind addresses not only the "sense" of this practice but also its
entire frame of reference, the form of life from which the reprehensible practice arises.[23] To put it pointedly, one then criticizes not
just the cruelty of the murders but also the superstition that fed it,
and the latter is criticized not just as superstition (or as a form of
ignorance) but as a technique of rule.[24] There is more that is
"wrong" here than the brutal persecution and murder of women
accused of witchcraft—practices that are "meaningful" in their
context to the extent that they are coherent and comprehensible.
What is "wrong" is the entire nexus, the paradigm, the very form
of life in the midst of which these practices stand and in terms of
which they must be understood. Here we see that complexes of
practices and beliefs cannot be overcome in the mode of refutation.
If progress concerns forms of life, and hence concerns the network
or ensemble in which these practices are situated, then forms of life
are not exempt from judgment; but they are not simply refutable,
nor can they be overcome purely through refutation.

5.3 Progress as process of enrichment

Let us assume that progress is determinable in a sense that does not
involve the blanket normative rejection of the practices and forms

of life that came before, the refutation of the "old meaning" on the basis of ahistorical criteria. We then need to understand the historical process in which those practices arise, erode, become obsolete, and displace each other as normatively substantive. If there is such a thing as progressive change in the sense I have proposed, it would consist neither in the elimination of mere normative errors, nor in a simple change in perspective from one "determinate sense" to another—neither of these would be progressive. Instead, such a change would have to address the imperfections, deficits, imbalances, blockages to learning, and contradictions of an existing social formation.

This brings me to the core of my conception, which seeks to draw on the dynamic of the change itself for criteria qualifying it as progressive or regressive. Progressive change, thus understood as a change that does not just "do away with the old meaning" but progressively overcomes it, is a *process of enrichment*. As such, it resembles the movement described in Hegel's *Phenomenology of Spirit*. The experiential process invoked by Hegel is one in which the object changes for consciousness, and with it the understanding that consciousness has of itself. This should be imagined neither as a disconnected, abrupt change in the object nor as its flat refutation. Rather, the experiential process is guided by an expanded understanding of the situation and the self, as well as by a correction of self-deceptions and biases. In a sense, the situation is redefined and overcome with reference to a more comprehensive situation in which it is embedded, or with reference to shortcomings in the previous description. What is new, the progress, the progressive situation, is then the result of a practically accomplished meta-reflection on what came before and how it was handled.[25] More than an improvement, progress becomes a reflexive enlargement of experience involving an increase in complexity, whereas regression would entail a loss of complexity and falling below a set level of reflexivity.

The process of enrichment should thus not be imagined as linear: it is mediated by crises and episodes of crisis management. The forms of experience described by Hegel (which could equally be understood as formations of practices) fall victim to their experiences if they fail to transform themselves. But enrichment should also not be understood in quantitative terms, akin to filling a glass of water, as some fear.[26] Enrichment processes in this eminently dialectical sense always contain a qualitative change. To stick with the image: the glass changes along with its contents. Understood in this way, the process by which experience is enriched can also be described with Dewey as an experiential history: crisis situations generate reflexivity, which opens up new options for action.[27] Reversing one of Walter Benjamin's motifs, experiences are made here that favor the making of experiences.[28] A pragmatically informed definition of progress would then be that progress amounts to an increase in experience, a crisis-induced growth in reflexivity. In Dewey, the concept of growth stands in for progress.[29] It denotes not only a *quantitative increase* in knowledge and experience but also a *qualitative intensification*. And growth, too, does not occur of its own accord (even if this is liable to misunderstanding) but is mediated by crises that have to be overcome reflexively—or via second-order problem-solving processes, as set out in Chapter 4.

Problem solutions are not simply successful if what had once been dysfunctional is restored to good working order. In that case, regressive solutions would also be functional, at least at first glance. But successful problem-solving involves more than just fine-tuning practices that have become meaningless or broken down and reintegrating them into a more or less well-oiled ensemble of practices. Where it can be described as successful, problem-solving occurs as a transformation in a mode of learning brought about by crises that compel new experiences and occasion new demands. Some of these transformations are continuous; others cannot happen without radical or revolutionary change. "Enrichment," "growth," and "successful learning" are hence a kind of procedural shorthand for what lies behind the idea of progress.

Once we consider the dynamic of progress from the pragmatist praxis-philosophical perspective I have proposed here—as a socio-historical experiential process threatened by blockages and up-heavals, and hence as a crisis-prone dynamic of *problem-solving attempts*—it becomes possible to evaluate the quality of the change *as* change. A social change is a *change for the better* because, and to the extent that, it is a *successful attempt at problem-solving*. It is not progressive because it moves toward a determinate (fixed, recognizable) solution or toward the good. In the event that the situation improves, it does so not because we are approaching a preestablished, normatively identified goal but because of the nature of the progress itself. It is this process, not its result, that helps us along philosophically. Untethered from any particular end, progress becomes a principle of movement in its own right.

A deflationary account of progress

So, while Ulrich may cast doubt on the possibility of determining progress, claiming that "there is no sense in our life as a whole," it turns out that there is a process-based alternative to the substantive determination of progressive goals (in both the global and local sense). In line with the primacy of progress developed in Chapter 1, "progress" is then not the problem but the solution that keeps us from falling into the metaethical dilemma outlined above. Whatever the chances may be of reaching philosophical agreement about the substantive objectives of human life or human societies, such a discussion misses our specific topic and the specific content of the concept of progress. It also misses its potential. If, in the light of the foregoing, we no longer wish to cling to a derivative, deontological or teleological account of progress, we will need to ask different questions. My proposal deflates the concept of progress in a specific way: not by confining it to a particular context, but by linking it to the overarching *form* of events in the sense of their dynamics, hence by taking as its criterion the quality of the learning process described above. This quasi-formal solution, and the orientation to problem-solving it entails, is neither "global" nor "local"; it concerns world history neither as a whole nor in its parts.

Even if "there is no sense in our life as a whole" and a goal of human development cannot be ascertained, we can still distinguish between the meaningful and less meaningful, the just and unjust ways in which sociohistorical forms of life unfold. The focus accordingly shifts from finding criteria for the goal of progress to finding criteria for the justice or injustice of a development that is either enriched by overcoming the problems and crises that affect and characterize a form of life or isn't.

Blockages to experience and problem-solving

These success criteria for a (self-enriching) experiential process derive from its opposite, the obstacles and barriers to this process, which I term blockages to experience. Problem-solving does not happen automatically and without hindrance. It can be impeded by power relations and is susceptible to systematic and structurally induced disruptions and blockages to learning. There are then good and bad, open and blocked, progressive and regressive problem-solving dynamics, as we will examine in Chapter 6.

In this respect, an absence of blockages to experience, including systematic blocks to seeing the problem in the first place, provides a negative yet reliable criterion for assessing successful problem-solving processes. Conversely, the ability to facilitate new experiences and an openness toward emerging problems and demands is a positive criterion for a rational and appropriate problem-solving process. We can distinguish between better and worse solutions without having to interpret the corresponding progress in metaphysical or teleological terms.[30] As indicated above, we can draw inspiration for such a conception from both Dewey's pragmatism and a Hegelian version of determinate negation. In this way, the question of success can be detached from any substantive determination of what constitutes the good life and directed toward the internal constitution of processes in which experiences are processed (in an emphatic sense), problems solved, and crises overcome.

Not the least of this account's merits is its pluralism. There are then several versions and possibilities for progressing successfully, just as there are many destructive variants of regression. And progress is always measured relative to different contexts—the problem-solving histories within which the respective dynamic plays out—without this depriving us of the ability to evaluate the histories themselves as more or less rational, more or less regressive.

The question of the *criterion* for progress has in fact made way for the question of whether this development is *progressive or regressive in its dynamic*. The short formula for progress that now presents itself reads: progress is whatever pertains to an ongoing, self-enriching problem-solving process, one that—negatively determined—is unimpeded by blockages and regressive episodes. Progress is a *self-enriching experiential process* in the sense that here experiences are made and conflicting experiences are not systemically blocked. A typology of such blockages to learning and regressive episodes—from ideological distortions and hermeneutical "lacunae" to the impoverishment of experience, alienation, and blockages to collective action—must then furnish the normative criteria that in my approach replace a positive description of the putative end point of progressive development.[31]

Progress as absence of regression

This is an essentially *negativist procedure*. The formal meta-category of non-regression issues from the non-teleological character of ori-

entation toward the dynamics of progress itself. This brings me to a
point that Adorno touches on in his short text on progress. If we
want to do justice to the dialectic of progress, the meaning of progress can only really be grasped from the concept of regression or
relapse:

> A situation is conceivable in which the category [of progress] would
> lose its meaning, and yet which is not the situation of universal re-
> gression that allies itself with progress today. In this case, progress
> would transform itself into the *resistance to the perpetual danger of
> relapse*. Progress is this resistance at all stages, not the surrender to
> their steady ascent [emphasis added].[32]

Progress is then neither—deterministically conceived—a quasi-
automatic development, nor does it depend on anticipating what
comes at the end of the "steady ascent," or having a predetermined
idea of what exactly a "rational establishment of the whole society
as humanity" might look like.[33] Resistance to instances of regression gains its shape and direction from the progressive and specific
determination of these very regressive instances.

As antonyms, the terms "progress" and "regress" illuminate the
complexity of the historical process we are trying to understand. If
progress is not just a linear forward march to a preestablished, positively valued end-state but an enrichment process, then regression
is not just a linear step backward but a relapse behind an already
attained position. It can be understood as a process of *unlearning*
in the sense of a systematic blockage to experience. Whereas
Habermas says that one cannot *not* learn, it now turns out that
empirically, a refusal to learn is perfectly possible. But there is a
price to pay for it in the form of regression. So, if progress is an
ongoing, self-enriching problem-solving process, then progressive
social movements and transformations are those that react appropriately to contradictions and crises, without an endpoint being
foreseeable or indeed necessary. Social change processes accordingly find a progressive as opposed to a regressive solution when

the new formation can be interpreted dialectically and pragmatically as responding rationally to an existing crisis (or existing problem).[34] Conversely, as I will explain in the next chapter, we can speak of regression where crises are not overcome, or where they are managed regressively.

5.4 Excursus: Dialectic of progress

As even the most committed defenders of progress will admit, progress can encounter setbacks. But these setbacks—the fact that a hard-won achievement can be wholly or partly, temporarily or permanently lost—do not seriously threaten the idea of progress. The problem of a "dialectic of progress," on the other hand, is more fundamental and likely to call into question the very idea of a progressive development.

As I pointed out in Chapter 1, the idea that progressive development is *linear* is based on the metaphor of a path. If you follow this path and continue along it, you will make progress; if you turn around and walk back the same way, you will regress. In other words, so long as you stay resolutely on track, things can only get better; and when they take a turn for the worse, it is because you reversed course until you moved behind what you had achieved. Even unexpected and unwelcome side effects of progress can be integrated into this conception, as byways and dead ends that should have been avoided but can always be retraced back to the main path.

In some respects, however, this is an oversimplified notion. The seeds of regression sometimes lie in progress itself. The quintessence of such a dialectic of progress is that we are dealing not only with reversals, ambivalences, unforeseen side effects, and willful misappropriations of a development that initially presented itself as progressive, but also with a development that is itself at best ambivalent, and at worst contradictory.

Progress as qualitative expansion of possibilities

In what sense, for example, is the transition from feudal to capitalist labor regimes progressive? Friedrich Engels's groundbreaking sociological study *The Condition of the Working Class in England* describes the suffering of the early industrial proletariat in England.[35] Upton Sinclair's novel *The Jungle* provides a similarly harrowing account of the living and working conditions endured by the migrants who toiled in Chicago's meat industry in the 1920s.[36] In terms of the abject misery, hopelessness, poor health, social neglect, and blatant exploitation they face, these workers are in some ways no better off than under conditions of feudal or unfree labor. There was a reason that Jack London described Sinclair's novel as the "*Uncle Tom's Cabin* of wage slavery,"[37] just as there was a reason that Marx castigated early capitalist working conditions as "white slavery."[38] If we draw on the quantitative indicators supplied by economists and philosophers to compare workers' "material quality of life" in early industrial capitalism and feudalism, we will find that conditions were more or less the same in both social formations, varying on a case-by-case basis. But what if material deprivation were perpetuated in many cases by the transition from unfree to, in Marx's words, doubly free labor?[39] What if relations of domination and dependency were merely placed on a more impersonal footing?[40] It could still be claimed (as Marx certainly claimed) that the replacement of unfree with "free" labor was a step forward.[41]

This argument can be made in a number of ways. Perhaps the most familiar is to distinguish between different dimensions or aspects of progress. Accordingly, the "condition of the working class" would have improved in one respect—that of formal equality before the law—but not necessarily (or not yet) in another, that of provision with material goods. Although clear progress has been made, this is at first restricted to legal formalities. Marx takes a different position. He presents wage labor as "a more refined and civilized means of exploitation" while nonetheless accepting that it represents an advance over slavery.[42] His point is that the replacement of a personal and direct form of exploitation by an indirect, more impersonal form, combined with the unleashing of productive forces under capitalism, has created the conditions for liberating workers both legally and materially from the chains of exploitation. Along with the development of the forces of production, the legal-formal shift from unfree labor to free wage labor is a change for the better insofar as it frees up opportunities for improving conditions across the board. This perspective differs significantly from the assumption that the change in legal status is inherently progressive, or even that it contains a "normative surplus" that will eventually bring improved material living conditions in its wake. The point is that Marx does not distinguish between two aspects here— one progressive, the other not (yet)—but places both sides in a relationship that is conducive to driving the "progressive" dynamic.

> It is one of the civilizing aspects of capital that it extorts this surplus labor [of wage laborers] in a manner and in conditions that are more advantageous to social relations and to the creation of elements for a new and higher formation than was the case under the earlier forms of slavery, serfdom, etc. Thus, on the one hand it leads toward a stage at which compulsion and the monopolization of social development (with its material and intellectual advantages) by one section of society at the expense of another disappears; on the other hand, it creates the material means and the nucleus for relations that permit this surplus labor to be combined, in a higher form of society, with a greater reduction of the overall time devoted to material labor.[43]

Of course, we do not have to agree with what Marx says about the "civilizing aspects of capital," which can be accused of whitewashing suffering—and real history has to some extent borne out this reproach. (For example, recent studies on violent accumulation and the violent history of capitalism, especially in its intertwining with slavery, give cause for skepticism here.)[44] What interests me here is Marx's line of argument, which reveals that progress is not always about achieving the good, or even always about achieving the better in a quantifiable sense. Progress means instead that a step has been taken toward unlocking the potential inherent in a given situation.[45] Movement has happened toward developing the conditions that enable a process of emancipation. This gives a further indication of what is meant by an enrichment process in the context of a dialectic of progress.

Emancipation of women

A good example of a much more complicated dialectic—perhaps one that pushes it to its limits—is provided by the changes in women's social position, living conditions, and legal status that have taken place over the past two centuries. The development from feudal society to the present is often told as a history of emancipation. The emancipation of the bourgeoisie, so the story goes, was followed by that of wage earners, who fought long and hard for political equality, social rights, and at least some degree of material security in modern bourgeois society. Beginning in the nineteenth century, and continuing into the twentieth, the legal subordination of women was also gradually, albeit haltingly, rectified. After the bourgeoisie and then the workers had taken up the fight for civil rights, the baton of emancipatory struggle was passed to women. With some delay, but following the same logic, and swept along by the same tide as these predecessor movements, women progressively achieved legal, formal, and material equality (the last imperfectly realized to this day). Notwithstanding the setbacks along the way, the achievements of this struggle are unmistakable, especially in recent decades.

This picture of progressively realized liberation is seductive but overly simplistic. Not only did bourgeois emancipation not do away with all forms of discrimination. Far more seriously, the abolition of one kind of discrimination—feudal-hierarchical society with its attendant forms of life and labor—gave rise to new and different forms of discrimination that disproportionately disadvantaged women. Put bluntly, women weren't just *not yet* treated as equals in the process of bourgeois emancipation; they were made unequal in a new way.

In broad outline, a counternarrative to the triumphalist tale of emancipatory progress and success reads something like this: as amply documented studies in gender history have shown, precisely at the moment when medieval corporatist distinctions fell away and political-legal equality became established as a normative ideal, sexually and biologically connoted differences become more important and virulent for collective and individual self-understanding.[46] Undine Eberlein puts it succinctly:

> In a heterogeneous premodern society organized along various hierarchical lines, . . . the nature "of woman" was not an especially pressing problem: integrated into vertically stratified ways of life, her "particularity" was only one aspect of a world structured according to God's will.[47]

While the premodern world was thus crisscrossed by multiple axes of inequality, only with enlightened modernity does the gender difference become entrenched as "the difference that makes a difference" (Gregory Bateson) when it comes to allocating social positions.

It is interesting to observe how the template for interpreting and legitimating gender relations shifts over the course of this change. With the Enlightenment and bourgeois emancipation, the "deficiency argument," according to which women are a lesser, incomplete version of generic humankind, is replaced by a dualistic "complementarity thesis," which states that men and women differ by nature and complement each other in their differences.[48] This thesis would radically reshape the living conditions of both men and women. Women were now no longer somehow deficient men but men's complementary other, emotionally supportive and nurturing helpmates whose place (where economically possible) was confined to the private sphere of the home.

From a historical perspective, the interpretive template based on a complementary duality of the sexes has not long been in force; it was by no means a mainstay of traditional or premodern forms of life. For all its claim to timeless validity, the supposedly natural way of things is a historically recent ideology.[49] And it serves, as Eberlein writes, to legitimize inequalities in gender relations:

> Despite various legal and social improvements, femininity thus became a category that established and justified the continued exclusion of women from the Enlightenment promise of equality. Even though the attribution of complementary characteristics to the sexes accorded women qualities of their own rather than declaring them to be merely "deficient," their classification in terms of a generally strict dichotomy meant that they were often more rigidly prevented from participating in "masculine" spheres, especially politics, than had been the case in premodern corporatist society.[50]

This shift is vividly illustrated in women's position in the workplace. Whereas in medieval times women had a publicly recognized role to play in both farming and craft production, the invention of housework and concomitant banishment of women from public life into domestic space is a modern development. As Barbara Duden and Gisela Bock have documented in their pioneering study on the genesis of housework, under conditions of an "economy of the entire household"—a smallholding or workshop that also included apprentices and journeymen—the work performed by women made them a visible part of the overall domestic economy.[51] Female labor was first pushed into the shadows by the changed economy of bourgeois society. With the specific division of labor ushered in by bourgeois capitalism, work processes were typically no longer vertically integrated within the house and farmyard or on the workshop floor but distributed across separate spheres. The associated attributions and divisions were then enshrined as an ideological-cultural ideal even in those (proletarian) class formations that could not afford such a separation. The "shadow work" that the women's movement has been problematizing since the 1970s is accordingly not an unwanted relic of premodern oppression but a product of the modern bourgeois world.[52] The emancipation of women has thus not gone hand in hand with the emancipation of society from feudal bondage. If anything, the opposite is the case, inasmuch as we have here a genuinely new form of exclusion, one that in its specificity is the product or even obverse of Enlightenment and bourgeois emancipation itself. Consequently, this development should not be understood as a basically linear movement with occasional setbacks, detours, and delays.

Eberlein writes that "the supposedly traditional idea of a strict gender dualism . . . is in many respects an 'achievement' of the Age of Enlightenment."[53] If so, and if it first brought forth and consolidated new relations of domination and exclusion, then we can only conclude that there was *neither progress nor regression* in gender relations under conditions of bourgeois emancipation. The situation of women changed in the age of the "dual revolution"—one political, the other industrial.[54] But rather than better or worse, it was primarily *different*. Exploitation and domination were not abolished; they merely assumed a new form. There was neither a great leap forward, nor did people simply turn around on the path of progress and take a few steps back. The idea that there are two separate paths, with progress being made on one but not the other, does not adequately describe the situation either. Instead, progress has produced *as its obverse* a frame of reference that has given a new ideological underpinning to the subordinate position of women in society. This was a *systematic* by-product of the social progress that came from dismantling feudal hierarchies.

Ambivalence or obverse?

So, in this case, are there merely changes that need to be analyzed, but in relation to which no progress—neither progress nor regression—can be discerned? My answer, a firm "no," involves a few steps.

Clearly, both the premodern theory of female deficiency and the modern theory of a complementarity between the sexes are inimical to women, limiting their standing and opportunities in life. (One could always argue about the quantitative extent of the oppression bound up with each theory, but this would be a waste of time.)

It is worth emphasizing, though, that the newly instituted form of male domination and exploitation is qualitatively *different* to what preceded it under feudalism. The bourgeois subjection of women is quite unlike the pre-bourgeois version. That is the decisive point. We are dealing with different forms of domination based on different conditions and involving different associated practices; moreover, each gender regime invites different possibilities for subverting or overcoming it. This point must be stressed against simplistic interpretations that identify an unchanging behemoth called patriarchy as the root of all evil.

In order to recognize a process of enrichment in all this, we need to take seriously the motif of the *obverse* mentioned above. In concrete terms, this means systematically correlating the ideology of gender dualism to the emergence of the bourgeois idea of equality. The naturalization of gender differences would then be a reaction to the idea of equality under natural law. As such, it was a particular answer to a particular constellation, albeit one that, in its very one-sidedness, created a momentous new division.

First, the natural-law concept of equality seems to require that there be something like naturally occurring inequality if gender can no longer define social status in an egalitarian civic order. The new form in which women are excluded and disempowered as the complementary "other" of men would be the obverse of the new equality enjoyed by all men (at least before the law). Second, according to this complementary logic, the "cold" and mechanistic new socioeconomic order needs the intimacy created by women as its "warm" counterpart. Or, following Hegel's interpretation of *Antigone*: the male bourgeois world has expelled and posited as its other precisely what is essential to its constitution.

The new dualism of the sexes is therefore an ideological model that both suits the new (material) conditions and is systematically produced by them. The new forms are not just new and different; they are themselves reactions to changing circumstances. They represent a solution to problems, whereby the solution and the problem (as always) are closely interconnected.[55]

Gaining a normative-historical sense of direction from such a narrative necessitates bringing the order of feudal differentiation and that of bourgeois equality into a common frame of reference. This, in turn, requires that we understand the newly instituted material constellation as one that has emerged from the contradictions and crises of the foregoing social formation. The obvious way to push for further progress—and this is the path that later emancipation movements have in fact taken—is to insist on full modern equality while developing complementary practices of solidarity with other social groups. Taking our cue from Marx's thesis about unlocking the potential for achieving the better, we might ask whether the assumption of equality under natural law is more conducive to this than the idea it replaced of a world structured according to God's will.

While a strict logic and dialectic of history would suggest that the "complementarity" version of patriarchy is a necessary step on the path to real equality, meaning that no path leads directly from the premodern situation to true inclusion, the deflationary understanding of a pragmatist-dialectical logic of enrichment processes that I am proposing leads to hidden but missed historical opportunities which, had they been grasped, would have brought about a change for the better. The French Revolution offers examples of such possibilities, including the Society of Revolutionary Republican Women: founded by Claire Lacombe, it campaigned for gender equality until it was forcibly disbanded in 1793.

6

BETRAYAL OF THE POSSIBLE

On the Anatomy of Regression

> The quest for an age past not only fails to indicate the way home but forfeits all consistency; the arbitrary conservation of the obsolete compromises what it wants to conserve, and with a bad conscience it obdurately opposes whatever is new.
> —THEODOR W. ADORNO

> What can be observed here is a flight from reality, but such a flight is commonplace at a time when so many feel almost indecently assaulted by reality. —GEORG DIEZ

PROGRESS, WE HAVE found, is a self-enriching learning process. In negative terms, progress denotes an absence of regression. But what is regression? I propose that it be seen as a blockage to learning and hence as a deficient mode of crisis management and problem solving. If processes of social transformation that can be understood as appropriate reactions to contradictions and crises are progressive, we may speak of regression, conversely, where crises are not overcome or are managed regressively. Just as progress, as I understand it, does not require an objective, regression should not be confused with falling behind a predetermined, fixed goal.

But what exactly is meant by "regressive crisis management"? Like the concept of progress, the concept of regression has multiple implications that are neither self-explanatory nor easy to defend.[1]

In this chapter, I will briefly discuss how regression is theorized in psychoanalysis (6.1) before examining what is specific to the concept by distinguishing it from neighboring concepts (6.2). I then elaborate the critical content of the regression theorem on the basis of Adorno's analysis of fascism and nationalism as regressive phenomena (6.3). I next turn to two problems posed by the concept (6.4): Does the diagnosis of regression have to start out from a substantive model of successful development? And is the stance critics of regression take toward those they criticize tainted by paternalism? I conclude by evaluating my findings in terms of an understanding of regression as a deficient mode of crisis management and roadblock to learning (6.5).

6.1 Regression in psychoanalysis

While the concept of regression enjoys a high profile in *public* life, its *philosophical* contours are anything but clear.[2] For all its popularity in contemporary political discourse, the term gets bandied about with studied vagueness.[3] The concept of regression and its implications are rarely made the object of reflection. The phenomena sometimes grouped together under the heading of "regression" for the purpose of diagnosing (or denouncing) the ills of our times are not regressive *per se*, regardless of how threatening, disturbing, or false they may be. After all, they could equally be interpreted as a mere shift in hegemony, as a rearguard action in defense of the status quo, or as a devastating breakdown in the liberal-democratic order, without any need for a strong concept of regression. The concept of regression gives the tendencies I have just mentioned a specific interpretation that must first prove its worth through its analytic richness and precision. Regression, like progress, is an interpretive paradigm and narrative.

For an initial run-up to a socio-philosophical analysis of regression, it is worth turning to the core meaning of the concept of regression in the context where it gained lasting significance: psychoanalysis. Even if direct analogies between individual psychological and social phenomena do not hold (a society, after all, is not a subject writ large, a mega-subject), the structural elements of individual regression investigated in psychoanalytical theory can still be used heuristically to help us understand social regression.

In psychoanalytic terms, regression is "a process in which an individual or group abandons a previously attained level of psychological structure or functioning to return to a level of thinking, feeling, or acting in their life history that is earlier and/or less structured." In regressing, patients revert to childlike "and hence more primitive modes of experiencing and processing."[4] Individual regressive processes are triggered and motivated by unresolved conflicts, crises, or personal problems, sometimes also by traumatic experiences that are prevented from filtering through to consciousness in order to safeguard the ego. Regression thus comes with an inability to access alternative, more appropriate means of conflict resolution. As such, it is one of the mechanisms that block access to one's own life story, curtailing autonomy and impeding necessary transformations.[5] If progress in psychosocial development means arriving at a more complexly structured, more "grown-up" way of functioning, tackling conflicts as they arise with the conflict management skills acquired over the course of one's life so far, then regression means moving backward from that.

In psychoanalysis, interestingly, the term lacks the exclusively pejorative connotations that it has in political discourse. There are quite innocuous and even salutary "regression[s] in the service of the ego," partial regressions in friendships or romantic relationships and in art, as well as euphoric rushes of dissolution and intoxication.[6] Elements of regression can also facilitate the therapeutic process; according to psychoanalyst Michael Bálint, regression is an "important ally of therapy."[7] In a sense, then, regression comes in both pathological and non-pathological forms. Whether these are problematic or unproblematic (because they relieve stress, for example) depends on how they function in a given context. An entire suite of socially permitted pleasures act in this sense as "safety valves for pent-up emotions and instinctual urges" and as "periodic outlets."[8] Tightly circumscribed in both time and place, these exceptional pleasures promote normal social functioning, just as regression can aid the healing process as an "ally of therapy."

Regression only becomes problematic where neither this dual limitation and containment (to particular times and/or places) nor the "cunning" role played by regression in the service of a non-regressive normality may be detected. Regression in the pejorative sense is not an innocent return to an earlier form of behavior or a temporary, invigorating release from the confines of the self; it is a somehow inappropriate reaction to a problem that may not be fully conscious and might even be repressed. Seen in this light, regression lies in the price to be paid for embracing regressive patterns of behavior and processing mechanisms: the avoidance of a conflict or crisis and the refusal of the learning and adjustment process called for in a crisis situation.

What is wrong with this dynamic? Where is the problem in clinging to an earlier stage of development? The answer is that this type of rection, and the avoidance of reality that goes with it, makes it more difficult to resolve crises, overcome problems, and manage conflicts. Regression in this sense is problematic to the extent that it promotes substitutions that help suppress failure or the feeling of powerlessness. In short, regression perpetuates processes that destroy resources for a solution and ultimately create an artificial roadblock to practical autonomy—an inherently contradictory, self-undermining process.

Regression is not a random step backward. If patients who regress revert to earlier, more "childlike" ways of experiencing and processing things, then the earlier state to which they return is obviously not the original world of the child. Regression does not make a person a child again but rather someone who, forced on the defensive or overwhelmed by a pressing situation or confrontation, reappropriates childish reactions and behavioral patterns. In doing so, they are thrown back to infantile conflicts that filter how they experience the real conflicts they are facing. From a psychoanalytical point of view, regression thus "fails to indicate the way home" (as Adorno remarks in relation to regression in music).[9] This is because it seeks a path back to a place that no longer exists and can be revisited in the imagination as a home, a refuge, only at great psychological cost. We will reencounter these same structural characteristics when we turn now to how the concept can be applied in social theory.

6.2 Nostalgia, regression, relapse

What is the difference between regression in the social field and a conservative allegiance to the tried-and-tested? In what follows, I will distinguish the concept of regression from comparable reactionary impulses to articulate the internal grammar or anatomy of regression in the social field. I will also sound out possibilities for transferring the concept from psychoanalysis to social philosophy.

Nostalgia and regression

Regressive change is something more and different than having recourse to earlier conditions, or reverting to former customs, ideas, practices, and institutions. There is nothing inherently wrong or harmful in turning to the past for guidance or solace, whether this takes the form of conservative traditionalism or a nostalgic hankering for happier times. Indeed, there are even cases where a partial reprise—going *back* to the way things used to be done, breathing new life into defunct or long-dormant practices—may be deemed progressive. It is not necessarily a sign of regression when heirloom tomato or apple varieties are recultivated and the Slow

Food movement takes on the might of agribusiness. And when elementary schools draw on the wisdom of earlier village schools to merge different year levels into composite classes, it is a return, but surely not a regressive one. Such cases are not only unproblematic, they can even be viewed as learning processes. The return to past practice here clearly results from reflection on new experiences, on a newly emerged situation, or on the adverse effects of more modern or progressive practices. There is a growing awareness that reintroducing the assortment of tasty old varieties that had disappeared from supermarket shelves makes better ecological and culinary sense than importing tropical fruits from halfway around the world. Or the idea is gaining ground that children learn at their own pace and sometimes learn best from other children, an experience that mixed-age instruction takes into account. On the other hand, there are good reasons for *not* reintroducing corporal punishment and the sullen recitation of material learned by rote (but not necessarily understood).[10]

If there is nothing inherently anti-progressive or regressive about such examples, this is because they result from reflection on past experiences or from a reflective approach to current conditions. This is precisely what constitutes a process of experience and learning. Such recourse to bygone practices is an (all too rare) instance of enlightened progress that reflects on the consequences and side effects of certain processes, integrates this reflection, and adjusts the dynamics of change in the light of what has been experienced. The non-regressive reconnection with the old only succeeds here by simultaneously appropriating the new, and it occurs from the reflective perspective of overcoming past problems and becoming aware of new possibilities.

To be sure, there are regressive forms of orientation, as well, and these cases are instructive for our attempt to pinpoint the concept of regression. A longing for the "good old things," as extolled in the catalog of the German online retailer Manufactum, can certainly be said to have regressive traits.[11] The nostalgia attested here—an enthusiasm that extends to vintage light switches and the tactile quality of old telephone receivers and dials—is open to ideological manipulation. The real regressive element, however, lies less in the vogue for retro design than in the compensatory function exercised by bespoke craftsmanship, weighty materiality, and authenticity in an age of industrial mass production.

A similar pattern of regressive compensation and repression makes the *Heimatfilm*, a popular film genre from 1950s Germany that showed strapping lads courting blushing maidens against an idyllic rural backdrop, a good example for how collective regression works.[12] At first glance more silly than salacious, these films become problematic due to their social function. The key factors here are once again their compensatory function, their omissions, and what these entail: a blatant loss of touch with reality. Less important than what the *Heimatfilm* shows in its yearning for an intact and wholesome world is what it does *not* show: the piles of rubble, the victims, the misery, and the fact that the parents and grandparents of those hale and hearty youngsters had just destroyed synagogues and arranged for the mass transportation of Jews to concentration and extermination camps. What is decisive, then, are the experiences that these films pass over in silence and hence cover up; the promise of a return to normality in a period that was anything but normal amounts to a regressive attempt to deflect attention from the fact that the political and moral foundations of an entire era had been smashed to smithereens. Hannah Arendt reported observing similarly regressive phenomena of de-realization on her first trip back to Germany after the war: "Among the ruins, the Germans are sending each other postcards of churches and marketplaces, public buildings and bridges that no longer exist."[13]

The remark by Adorno cited in the epigraph to this chapter provides a clue to how the mechanism of regression works: "the arbitrary conservation of the obsolete compromises what it wants to conserve, and with a bad conscience it obdurately opposes whatever is new." This suggests a criterion for determining what makes recourse to past practices regressive rather than unproblematic. The problem does not lie in the nostalgic wish to hold on to the past. It begins where this "obdurately opposes" the new, or where it is deployed to avoid having to face up to aspects of reality that clearly cannot be endured and confronted head-on.

While there is nothing necessarily regressive about reviving past practices, a fixation on tradition can be classified as regressive when it appears as an inconsistent, arbitrary reaction to crisis-prone social changes or those perceived as such, indeed as a reaction that aggressively represses the reality of those changes. This is indicated by the compulsive quality and sometimes startling violence of the backlash to the change in question, as seen in the hate-filled global reaction in some quarters to shifts in family structures and gender norms. This reaction can be identified as regressive not just by the *contents* of the position adopted here but by the *functions* it performs in social life: compensation for and/or repression of an insoluble tension between known problems and the socially obstructed possibility of reacting to them in an appropriate way.

Not every step backward is regressive

As we have seen, clinging to tradition is not always a step backward. Moreover, not every backward step is regressive. A society can fall behind its moral or social achievements or repeal them without regressing in the specific sense I have in mind here. This is illustrated by some cases where retrograde tendencies have clearly prevailed. Let us assume that public health insurance or marriage equality were to be abolished and rights for asylum-seekers in Germany were drastically curtailed (again).[14] This would be a significant setback. Rights, practices, and institutions that many of us value, take for granted, or regard as important achievements would then no longer be available. A movement for change that had gathered momentum would be cut short and prevented from being fully realized. For many, this would no doubt be a painful and momentous change in social infrastructure that would dramatically restrict their opportunities in life, providing ample grounds for seeing this process as a step backward. But not every such step follows the pattern of social regression—even when it leads to broader processes of political restoration.[15]

At any time, relapses can interfere with the dynamics of social transformation and emancipation processes. They are even more likely to do so than not. Social progress often encounters obstacles; advances are stonewalled, stymied, stopped in their tracks. Faced with unexpectedly fierce resistance, progressive measures get bogged down in partisan rancor and infighting. Those who oppose a reform or innovation gain the upper hand. While these are unfortunate developments that can lead to temporary and local, longer- or medium-term setbacks, they do not preclude any chance of eventually implementing progressive measures under more propitious circumstances. What Donald Trump abolished can always be reinstated by a later president, at least in theory. Although the attempt to impose a rent cap in Berlin has failed for the time being, it could always be reintroduced. And many a winter of political restoration has given way to a springtime of reform. These relapses—and herein lies the crucial difference from regression—merely face *external obstacles*.

Regressive phenomena, on the other hand, always have an *immanent cause*. They are the expression of an internally driven crisis dynamic and an internally induced (mis)development. To return to one of my earlier examples, if the erosion of the European welfare state is interpreted as the symptom of a "regressive modernity," as Oliver Nachtwey has proposed,[16] then this does not just mean that some of the welfare state's achievements, such as the promise of social advancement through educational equality, have been relinquished. The diagnosis of regression relocates the problem firmly *within* the social formation. It is then claimed, for example, that the modern welfare state failed to evolve with the necessary reflexivity, since no appropriate institutional framework was found for dealing with its unintended side effects. As a result, the welfare state proved incapable of reconciling its key antagonisms and reflectively interrogating the systemic confines of the existing social security system, including its orientation to the model of the normal worker and the normal family, its problematic normalizing and disciplining effects, and its national limitations.[17]

All these aspects, which I allude to here solely for the purpose of illustration, result in society at least faltering before its self-made crises. The fact that the modern welfare state does not solve its own problems (or does not solve them quickly enough) does not make it regressive; it may be described as regressive if and when it *cannot* address them because its crisis tendencies are endemic to it. Access to solutions is then systematically blocked.[18] Similarly, the political tendency to authoritarianism would be regressive, and not just a relapse, if it could be shown that it does not imperil liberal democracy from without but undermines it from within. This development represents a self-induced crisis in liberal democracies and a reaction to existing structural deficits: a second-order problem that strikes at the heart of those democracies.

6.3 Fascism and nationalism as regression

The structure of social regression (and the concept of regression as a category of interpretation) is most vividly illustrated in the early Frankfurt School's analysis of fascism. Fascism is seen here as regressive, but certainly not as a mere relapse into premodern conditions. Benjamin's dictum, the "amazement that the things we are experiencing are 'still' possible in the twentieth century is *not* philosophical,"[19] could equally stand as motto to Adorno and Horkheimer's reflections in *Dialectic of Enlightenment*. Understood as regression, the descent into "barbarism"[20] is not a mere retreat behind the achievements of modernity, a turning back of the clock. On the contrary, fascism is a specifically modern phenomenon: "As a rebellion against civilization, fascism is not simply the reoccurrence of the archaic but its reproduction in and by civilization itself."[21]

According to Adorno and Horkheimer's analysis of regression, this is true not just because German National Socialism carried out the mass extermination of human life on an industrial scale and with the most modern logistical means at its disposal, but because it resulted from a misguided dynamic and from unresolved tensions and contradictions within capitalist modernity itself. Consequently, this "new kind of barbarism"[22] does not transport an earlier, archaic type of social organization into a different period. Far from going into reverse, the wheels of history roll on, albeit in the mode of a misdirected attempt to manage conflict. For these authors, fascist "barbarism" is therefore not an anthropological constant that expresses itself in periodic outbursts of atavistic, ahistorical violence.[23] It has a history of its own and is the result of a sociohistorical process. Fascist barbarism is a new, historically conditioned, yet distinctively *modern* phenomenon in which historical experiences are preserved and take effect, albeit in a regressive way. The example of National Socialism makes this crystal clear. The Nazis did not just hark back to an agrarian or premodern economy and lifestyle, something that could also have been done in a non-regressive way. Instead, they ramped up the development of a military-industrial complex while at the same time propagating a crassly biologistic, blood-and-soil ideology. They thus responded to the atomizing tendencies of modern industrial societies with an ideology and politics of reactionary communitarianism, not by forging the modern solidarities that were so urgently needed. Fascism counters the destabilizing experience of industrial modernity—the alienation and meaninglessness arising from new forms of anomie—

with a sense of security and belonging seemingly guaranteed by ancestry, tradition, and racial integrity. But this, following Adorno, is an inadequate mechanism for managing crises and an inappropriate way to process experience—with well-known consequences.

Regression to ethnonationalism

These regressive patterns of denial of experience can be pursued further in Adorno's critical analysis of nationalism, characterized in his lectures on history and freedom as a deficient mode of social experience.[24] According to Adorno, nationalism regressively insulates itself from the demands posed by the real cosmopolitanism of the bourgeois-capitalist economy. Adorno's starting point is the simultaneously progressive and regressive function of the nation-state. As political artifacts, nation-states emerged artificially from the dissolution of earlier polities structured along kinship lines. The nation, as Adorno emphasizes, is thus not something (naturally or primordially) *given* but (politically) *made*. Nations are "imagined communities," in Benedict Anderson's terms.[25] From Adorno's perspective, the emergence of nation-states represents an emancipatory advance over organic, familial communities based on blood ties.[26] Paradoxically, however, nationalism denies precisely this artificial, political character of the nation. Its very lack of a natural foundation makes it insist on one all the more adamantly:

> Precisely because the nation is not nature, it has ceaselessly to proclaim its closeness to nature, its immediacy and the intrinsic value of the national community.[27]

Symptomatic of the regressive character of the nation is the doggedness with which the contingency of its institution, its unnatural quality, has to be denied and concealed. It is only fitting, then, that the "fetishism of the nation is especially highly developed in countries where nation-building was a failure."[28] This fetishism festers

into violence and aggression, and not just when it reaches a geno-
cidal extreme.

How does the regressive structure I am interested in reveal itself
here? Denial of experience and resulting blockage have two dimensions. On the one hand, naturalization involves a denial that na-
tionhood is a construct, a flight into an imaginary nature. Rather
than taking responsibility for a shared social space of human
making, it hypostatizes an ethnic identity that is sealed off to out-
siders. We are dealing here with a category error with regard to the
status of the entity in question, an error that, precisely because it
flies in the face of real social experience, can only be upheld by dint
of massive and sustained denial. On the other hand, regression
manifests itself in denial of the historically real, factual obsolescence of the nation-state paradigm. The regression here consists in
continued adherence to ethnonationalism in spite of objective
transnational interdependence, and hence also to a model of sovereignty that has long since been hollowed out. What once had a
function—even an emancipatory one—and corresponding problem-
solving capabilities has now forfeited them.[29] Clinging to traditional understandings and institutions regressively hinders confrontation with this reality and the broad process of working through
problems.

In both respects, then, one can see the nationalism that Adorno
had in mind as a loss of reality and systematic denial of experience.
As a result, the level of problem-solving already attained and the
problem-solving skills already acquired (here: the dissolution of
kinship associations) are undermined and the problems at hand—
the task of democratic self-determination in view of the loss of national sovereignty and global economic interpenetration—can no
longer be posed or adequately addressed.[30] Writing about developments in his time, Adorno describes this in terms that resonate
strikingly with our own:

> It is no longer the case that so-called cosmopolitanism is the more
> abstract thing in contrast to the individual nations; cosmopolitanism

now possesses the greater reality. We can now see a convergence in countless forms of life . . . [that] points to the convergence of the fundamental processes of life, in other words, the dominance of industrial production.[31]

Whence the following task:

So today, the task is not simply to preserve the concrete essence of human relations in the transitory form of the different nations—which incidentally has long been unmasked as fraudulent—but to bring about this concrete state of human community on a higher plane.[32]

Referred back to my terminology of problems posed and deficiently addressed: the problem does not present itself solely as a normative demand (for cosmopolitanism) but arises from the factual convergence of living conditions. The more appropriate experiential and learning process that is so desperately needed but obstructed by the regressive adherence to the nation, and even more so by the regression to ethnonationalism, would then consist in realizing this new "concrete state of human community"—today we would perhaps speak of a "solidaristic belonging" or even a "community of the unchosen"—on a "higher plane."[33]

Regression as defensive re-naturalization

The parallels between the situation analyzed by Adorno and our current predicament are hard to ignore. Those on the right tend to resurrect anti-Semitic tropes by accusing the liberal left of cosmopolitan rootlessness (pitting the "somewheres" against the "anywheres").[34] But the roots to which they themselves clutch have long since crumbled into dust.[35] The same pattern of regression as a defense against crisis and roadblock to learning seems to be in play in the resistance shown by the populist-authoritarian right to changing gender norms and family structures. Ostentatiously clinging to the traditional family unit and "natural" gender relations, they conjure up the specter of social and moral collapse in the face of a bewildering profusion of genders, personal pronouns, and choose-your-own identities and lifestyles.[36] Perhaps harmlessly conservative in some cases, this populist backlash becomes both aggressive and regressive the more it denies the reality of a changing society. It is obvious that the "good old family" and traditional order of the sexes cease to be the default position once they have been stripped of their aura of naturalness. As soon as the traditional family model is no longer taken for granted, becoming merely one option among many, the family has already changed irrevocably. The fact that aggressive reactions in these contexts, including even the urge to wipe out alternative ways of life, are openly expressed and turned into a political platform can only be interpreted as ressentiment-fueled regression.[37] What is unquestionably apparent here is a (regressive) longing for naturalized certainties, a return to a state of undisputed classifications and boundaries, and a fear of losing the ground beneath one's feet—a "fear of freedom."[38]

The reality-denying defense against critical changes that are experienced as threatening can be described more precisely with the help of the multidimensional interpretation of the dynamics of social change sketched in Chapters 3 and 4. Changes in family structure and gender relations are anything but trivial in economic, social, and cultural respects. An entire structure of social practices and institutions is in flux, a whole complex of self-conceptions and perceptions that reaches deep into the socialization (or, in more modern parlance, subjectivation) of individuals. It is not just ideas that are caught up in this process of change, but an extensive network of social practices with diverse effects on the (normative) reproduction of the societies affected. Once one recognizes how many different factors contribute to them, it becomes clear that the changes could not have been brought about either by the "gender madness" denounced in authoritarian, neo- and proto-fascist circles or by the campaigners for plural, no-longer-heteronormative families. It is not only the attitudes and wishes of individual and social groups that have changed, but equally the socio-structural conditions under which they lead their lives. This seismic shift has been enabled, necessitated, facilitated, or at least made more likely by profound transformations in the organization of labor and in other aspects of the way we live, not least in technological conditions and media communications. Active and passive elements thus go hand in hand, as set out above.

This then provides the starting point for an analysis of regression. The hateful reaction directed at protagonists of progressive or emancipatory movements is regressive because it fails to do justice to the complex depth dimension of events. The inadequate reaction to a social shift and to social crisis dynamics is regressive because the problem cannot be effectively addressed by assigning responsibility to incriminated groups. If progress is "change within change," regression is "regressive change within change": a deficient reaction to change that stands in the way of an adequate, realistic, interventionist confrontation with real processes of change.

6.4 Problems with the concept of regression

Regression, I have suggested, is a blockage to experience triggered by unresolved crises or problems that makes itself felt through the attempt to revert to earlier developmental stages.[39] One could object that, by drawing on a psychoanalytic interpretive paradigm, two problems bound up with the traditional concept of progress reemerge: the problem of a developmental logic and the problem of paternalism.

Developmental logic

Turning first to the problem of a developmental logic: regression, understood as a relapse behind an achieved level of complexity, seems to be tied to a stage model of development that is problematic when applied to social and historical phenomena. And it is clear that the concept of regression elaborated above also assumes a sequence of events that build upon each other. Talk of accumulation (or enrichment) and decumulation (or depletion) suggests that social experiences react to each other or follow on from each other, either in a productive, self-enriching way or in an unproductive, if not downright destructive, one.

But if regression can be understood by analogy to my process-based concept of progress, this does not imply that such a process can and must have a definitive endpoint, or that it unfolds in teleological fashion, such that the goal of the completed process is already contained, germ-like, in its inception. The dynamic of transformation I am presupposing here results from the fact that every social order solves problems and can thereby become embroiled in crises to which it reacts in one way or another. The reason why regression is not an arbitrary relapse is that the conditions we are examining here have taken on their current form by emerging from and displacing each other. Precisely in this succession or supersession, they react—however inadequately—to the specific deficits of the preceding situation. There is a sequence of erosions and transformations of social institutions and practices, which is why regression can be understood analogously to progress as a process that can be used to identify deficits or distortions within such crisis-prone problem-solving dynamics.

In defense of such a formal and non-teleological process of enrichment, it may be informative if we go back to psychoanalysis. To ascertain the appropriateness or inappropriateness of such a developmental process, does psychoanalytic theory in general or the individual therapist have to set a precisely defined developmental objective? These are controversial questions within psychoanalytic theory that cannot and need not be discussed exhaustively here. Nonetheless, a psychoanalytic approach can lend support to the proposal for a dialectical but non-teleological experiential and learning process sketched in Chapters 4 and 5.

Here we can make a direct link to Freud. Translated into philosophical terminology, the psychoanalytic cure can be understood as aiming at freedom (or emancipation) rather than happiness or the attainment of a determinate, substantively describable state. In a nutshell, psychoanalysis is interested in doing away with obstacles to action and compulsive distortions and fixations; it aims to restore to the analysand access to their own feelings and to no-go areas in their own life story.[40] A key psychoanalytic insight is that we are not "masters in our own house" but are influenced in our actions and orientations by unconscious impulses and mechanisms that escape our rational control.[41] In light of this, the aim is to make us capable of taking action, even if untrammeled autonomy and self-transparency will remain forever beyond our grasp. It is about clearing away whatever impediments stand between us and our own desires and impulses. The goal, mental health, can then no longer be described in substantive terms as a positive state of mind; much like my process-based concept of progress, it can only be described formally, as a way of relating to the world and the self that is characterized by a basic self-accessibility and the possibility of identifying with others and the other (the social and objective world). Freud seems to have had something similar in mind when he declared the ability to love and work to be the goal of therapy and what he took mental health to mean. Put differently, psychoanalysis sets out to restore the capacity—but also the will and the motivation—to appropriate one's environment, to cathect objects libidinally, to set oneself in relation to them, and thus to experience oneself as a self-empowered agent, the source of a stance toward the world that is at once active and resonant (as Hartmut Rosa would say).

What particularly interests me in how Freud defines the goal of psychoanalysis is its open-endedness: it involves finding (and constantly recalibrating) a way of relating to oneself and one's own activities, capacities, and desires. After all, being able to love and work is not a goal tied to any particular content but a mode of living, one in which we identify and engage meaningfully with what we do within a shared objective world. The latter is taken to form part of a malleable and fundamentally accessible experiential space in which we equally come to terms with what *cannot* be changed, the limits to our independence as human beings. In essence, this entails a basic capacity for (relational) autonomy or self-determination in reciprocity.[42] It does not guarantee a happy or even successful life. As mentioned earlier, such a developmental goal cannot be specified by means of concrete, substantive qualities. It can only be understood as a mode of relating to the world and the self that involves a certain awareness and constant juggling of crises and conflicts, tensions and ambiguities, separations and experiences of loss. Access to the world and the self in the mode of generalized (albeit moderated) agency contrasts with modes of regressive avoidance and hence inaccessibility.[43] Here, too, progress in maturity or mental health would not mean moving ever closer to a substantive developmental goal; it denotes an absence of regression that can take quite different forms. Conversely, regression does not mean moving further away from a developmental goal but rather failing to achieve a particular mode of experiencing the world and the self.

Paternalism

The second problem follows on from the first. A paternalistic streak seems to run through the interpretive paradigm of regression to the extent that it purports to look down in judgment on the positions of social actors. This can be best be explained by comparing it with the very different interpretive paradigm of hegemony. What is the outcome if the rise in authoritarian tendencies and growing hostility to processes of cultural liberalization is understood either as a gain (or loss) in *hegemony* on the part of certain social groups or as *regression*?

According to the interpretive paradigm of hegemony, fascist-authoritarian-populist tendencies could have brought about a shift in hegemonic discourse as well as enforced a recasting of positions of power; on this view, racist, misogynist, or homophobic groups would then have clawed back the influence they had once (almost) lost.[44] Perceptible shifts in discourse and actual setbacks—the collapse of what had been partially achieved—would accordingly result from one social group or interest group defeating another in a struggle for power. Regression analysis, by contrast, adopts a broader perspective. It focuses less on the shift in hegemonic interests and contestation of privileges than on the crisis that underlies them. It sees the root cause of those power shifts in a development that encompasses the conflicts in question and first makes it possible for a recrudescent ethnonationalism to regain the ascendancy. In other words, where an analysis of hegemony registers antagonisms, the regression narrative sees crises and dysfunctionalities, social malaise, and a form of irrationality at work.

What is at stake here? From the perspective of hegemony theory, it could be argued that the development I have been describing is not a general crisis that affects everyone. It is only a disadvantage for some, above all those impacted by racism, sexism, social exclusion, and precarity, and an advantage for others. Progress for the winners would then be regression for the losers, disqualifying any interpretation of events from a higher vantage point. In contrast, the regression-theory position sees more going on here than one group gaining the upper hand at another's expense. This is not a zero-sum game—an entire society has fallen into a pathological state or is so constituted that it can no longer react meaningfully to the experiences that press upon it. Put differently, the concept of regression assumes that there is in some sense a *common situation*, not just various competing and colliding interest groups. The accusation of paternalism made against regression analysis is that it pathologizes instead of taking up arms, that it seeks therapeutic reasons instead of recognizing and combating antagonistic interests, and hence that the respective "other side," but also the situation as a whole, is not taken seriously enough.

Yet the regression narrative hardly denies that different social groups can emerge from a crisis with very different advantages and disadvantages. It agrees that not everyone is in the same boat—or at least, they are berthed on different decks. In other words, although regression affects the course of the entire ship, it has different consequences for different actors. There are thus winners and losers within regression processes, too. Racism and ethnonationalist ideologies benefit certain social groups in asserting their claims to cultural and political dominance; "anti-genderism" and the "war on woke" benefit (cis-gender) men who are hell-bent on maintaining their privileges; the deregulation of social infrastructure has quite different impacts in different social settings. This is clearly also a question of power relations.[45] But that is not to say that these developments could not also be *wrong in a regressive sense*. Resorting to "biology" when confronted with obvious and necessary changes to family structure, reacting to global economic integration and the pressing task of fashioning a global welfare state with a nationalism that seeks to address problems that cannot be solved at the national level, and upholding the imagined values of culturally or ethnically homogeneous societies in view of real threats to social solidarity, can succeed only at the cost of massive violence toward others, but also toward oneself. If all this is not just a move in a chess game of social power but a sign of social irrationality—the kind of irrationality I call *regression*—then this position denies neither conflict nor violence. Instead, it explores the conditions for overcoming them in a different way.

6.5 Regression as inappropriate crisis reaction and learning disorder

From what has been said so far, some conclusions may be drawn for the concept of regression that are germane to the analysis of social relations. First and foremost, regression is a reaction, not a position. It is not a substantively positive stance but a repudiation of social dynamics experienced as upsetting, vexing, and disorienting. In the political domain, regressive positions should not be confused with a conservative allegiance to the past.[46] Regression is an attempt to conserve something that cannot be conserved, to return somewhere to which there can be no return. Regression reacts to a problem with petulant outrage; it shrugs off a crisis with denial. It is an inappropriate processing of problems, a mode of unlearning and blockading experiences—a flight from (inner and outer) reality.

Regressive episodes are based on *internal, self-generated, and systematic blockages to development*; they are an expression of inhibited learning or experiential processes and of deficient ways of dealing with crises. In contrast to the enrichment that comes from a successful experiential process, regression is depletion and impoverishment. A successful learning process always contains an element of *learning how to learn*.[47] It could also be said of regressive processes that they involve *unlearning* how to learn. The regressive way of processing experience is not only inappropriate in relation to the current situation; as an avoidance strategy, it blocks the possibility of further experience on which the prospect of change depends.

Regression is hence a *crisis in resolving crises*, a second-order problem. It is not the inability to manage a crisis or solve a problem. Regression sets in where the means to perceive and solve problems have already been systematically destroyed and made inaccessible. Crises are then not only *unresolved*, but cannot even be adequately articulated, addressed, and—crucially for the dynamics of social transformation processes—turned into conflicts, or at any rate not in an appropriate way.

To speak of regression therefore does not mean wanting to hold on to the *status quo ante*, the pre-regressive state. While one might strive to restore the former state—to reverse the reversion—in the case of a simple setback, this would clearly be futile in the case of regressive phenomena, since the causes of regression are to be found in that very former state. A regressive tendency is thus not only not a backward step, but it also cannot be eliminated by stepping back from the backward step. Regression is part of a broader crisis scenario that must be addressed at the root of the given crisis. If we are currently experiencing something like a "democratic regression," the solution cannot simply lie in returning to the democracy we had before.[48] Unlike a temporary setback, the reaction to a regressive process cannot be to rally the troops around one more push to recover lost ground. Regression affects the practice and possibility of making renewed headway. That is why it takes more than the resumption of "business as usual" to overcome regression, and that is why the reaction to a regressive development must consist in reflecting and working through the immanent causes of regression.

Progress is irreversible, we sometimes hear. *Empirically*, this is a bedtime story told to soothe frightened children. As comforting as it would be if certain social achievements turned out to be irreversible, given what Hegel called the "bloodbath" of world history, it is more than doubtful that there are any empirical "barriers to regression" (Habermas) to keep us from falling behind an achieved state. *Criterially*, however, as Habermas argued, progress is indeed irreversible in some respects. If the sound and the fury of world history is not simply a backlash but a symptom of regression, then there is indeed something like a barrier to regression—but in an altogether different, less Panglossian sense. One can always move back to an earlier level, but *not without consequences*. If we assume a process of experience and learning, then regressive unlearning or regressive stagnation is worse than learning nothing at all. The real point of Habermas's claim that we "cannot *not* learn" is that progress may well be reversible, but only at a great cost.[49] Regression behind an achieved state is worse than the situation before the relapse or the situation to which one supposedly wants to return. The Nazi blood-and-soil ideology is worse than the premodern "idiocy of rural life" disparaged by Marx and Engels.[50] And likewise, the aggressive communitarianism of the new right is worse than the hidebound traditionalism of an established in-group.

In precisely this sense of a normative-criterial barrier to regression, history does not just seesaw up and down. Nor is it simply caught up in the throes of perpetual change, without any identifiable sense of direction. The costs of regression can be tallied—and from this tallying, the ways that things would have been or could have been better can be discerned.

Fascism as regression is more than just morally evil, I argued in dialogue with the early Frankfurt School. As we have seen, regression is a kind of inappropriate relation to reality—that is, a failure to come to grips with emerging crises. The key impulse for engaging with the concept of regression is that it opens up space for explanatory and analytical questions. The diagnosis of regression requires us to burrow down to the causes of crises and to those systemic and structural problems that trigger and motivate regressions. In short, like "progress," "regression" is not a solely normative concept. It is not entirely bound by the horizon of Kant's "practical question" of *What ought we to do?* Instead, it is aimed at the social and structural conditions, contingencies, and consequences of our actions. In this sense, it is a typical and indispensable tool of a critical theory.

Those who side with the forces of regression are "betraying the possible," Adorno writes.[51] Rather than simply falling behind, they "would like best to root out the nagging possibility" that things might be different. They therefore stand in the way of emancipatory change. If progress and regression are both modes of change within change, they nonetheless mark an alternative between appropriate and inappropriate ways of addressing the tendencies, contradictions, crises, and conflicts inherent in the existing order. "Socialism or barbarism" was Rosa Luxemburg's very clear and, alas, not entirely dated translation of that alternative.[52]

NOTES

Preface

Epigraphs: Peter Kurzeck, *Peter Kurzeck erzählt: Unerwartet Marseille* (Frankfurt: Schoeffling / Stroemfeld, 2019).
Dietmar Dath, *Maschinenwinter. Wissen, Technik, Sozialismus* (Frankfurt: Suhrkamp, 2008), 13.

1. Anne Robert Jacques Turgot, "Plan de deux Discours sur l'Histoire Universelle," in *Oeuvres de Turgot et documents le concernant*, ed. Gustave Schelle (Paris: Félix Alcan, 1913), vol. 1, 285. Author's translation.

2. See Maximilian Pichl, *Der "Moria-Complex": Verantwortungslosigkeit, Unzuständigkeit und Entrechtung fünf Jahre nach dem EU-Türkei Abkommen und der Einführung des Hotspot-Systems* (Frankfurt am Main: Medico International, 2021); Bernd Kasparek, *Europas Grenzen: Flucht, Asyl und Migration* (Berlin: Bertz + Fischer, 2019).

3. President Joseph R. Biden, State of the Union Address, Washington, DC, February 7, 2023.

4. Steven Pinker, *Enlightenment Now: The Case for Reason, Science, Humanism, and Progress* (New York: Viking Penguin, 2018).

5. Ashis Nandy, "Two Hundred Years of Silence," *Le Monde Diplomatique*, October 2015, https://mondediplo.com/2015/10/14supp.

6. Glen Sean Coulthard, *Red Skin, White Masks: Rejecting the Colonial Politics of Recognition* (Minneapolis: University of Minnesota Press, 2014), 11.

7. Quoted in Amy Allen, *The End of Progress: Decolonizing the Normative Foundations of Critical Theory* (New York: Columbia University Press, 2016), 3.

8. In 2017, for example, a volume of essays appeared in which leading international theorists, responding to Donald Trump's election as president and a worldwide increase in authoritarian and populist right-wing movements, diagnosed a "Great Regression." See Heinrich Geiselberger, ed., *Die große Regression: Eine internationale Debatte über die geistige Situation der Zeit* (Berlin: Suhrkamp, 2017). More recently, Michael Zürn and Armin Schäfer have discussed the same problems under the heading of "democratic regression": *Die demokratische Regression: Die politischen Ursachen des autoritären Populismus* (Berlin: Suhrkamp, 2021).

9. See also Sabine Hark and Sighard Neckel, "Kulturelle Ressourcen: Sighard Neckel und Sabine Hark im Gespräch über Ressentiments und Rachegefühle," *Texte zur Kunst* 106 (2017), 42–46.

10. Jonathan Friedman and Nadine Farid Johnson, "Banned in the USA: The Growing Movement to Censor Books in Schools," *PEN America at 100*, September 19, 2022, https://pen.org/report/banned-usa-growing-movement-to-censor-books-in-schools/.

11. Nachtwey characterizes the neoliberal tendency to generate precarious working conditions and undermine the institutions of the welfare state as the effect of a "regressive modernity." At the same time, a new type of authoritarian character has emerged in the "regressive rebel." See Oliver Nachtwey, trans. L. Balhorn and D. Fernbach, *Germany's Hidden Crisis: Social Decline in the Heart of Europe* (London: Verso, 2018), and Nachtwey and Maurits Heumann, "Regressive Rebellen: Konturen eines Sozialtyps des neuen Autoritarismus," in *Konformistische Rebellen: Zur Aktualität des autoritären Charakters,* eds. Katrin Henkelmann et al. (Berlin: Verbrecher, 2020). On the precariat, see Guy Standing, *The Precariat: The New Dangerous Class*, 2nd ed. (London: Bloomsbury, 2021).

12. Jean-Paul Sartre, trans. Hazel E. Barnes, *Being and Nothingness* (New York: Washington Square Press, 1984), 86–118, 86.

13. As Adorno writes: "Progress wants to cut short the triumph of radical evil, not triumph as such itself." Theodor W. Adorno, trans. Henry W.

Pickford, "Progress," in *Critical Models: Interventions and Catchwords* (New York: Columbia University Press, 2005), 143–160, 160. The term "Whig history" goes back to Herbert Butterfield, *The Whig Interpretation of History* (New York: Norton, 1965). Butterfield criticizes its view of history as progress, especially the tendency to project contemporary attitudes and values onto the past.

14. Theodor W. Adorno, trans. A. Rabinbach, "On the Fetish-Character in Music and the Regression of Listening," in Adorno, *Essays on Music,* ed. R. Leppert (Berkeley: University of California Press, 2002), 288–317.

15. [The German term for "concept" used here, *Begriff*, is cognate with the verb "to grasp" (*begreifen*).—Translator's note.]

16. Along these lines, Amy Allen has proposed distinguishing between two senses of progress: progress as fact and progress as ideal. Allen rejects the former and embraces the latter. On this distinction, see Allen, *The End of Progress*, 12.

17. Karl Marx and Frederick Engels, *The German Ideology: Part One,* ed. C. J. Arthur (New York: International Publishers, 1970), 57.

18. Adorno, *Critical Models*, 148.

19. I am thinking primarily of Elizabeth Anderson's pathbreaking work. See, for example, Elizabeth Anderson, "The Social Epistemology of Morality: Learning from the Forgotten History of the Abolition of Slavery," in *The Epistemic Life of Groups: Essays in the Epistemology of Collectives,* eds. Miranda Fricker and Michael Brady (Oxford: Oxford University Press, 2016), 75–94; Elizabeth Anderson, "Social Movements, Experiments in Living, and Moral Progress: Case Studies from Britain's Abolition of Slavery," Lindley Lecture, University of Kansas, February 11, 2014. See also Kwame Anthony Appiah, *The Honor Code: How Moral Revolutions Happen* (New York: Norton, 2010); Philip Kitcher, *The Ethical Project* (Cambridge, MA: Harvard University Press, 2011); Philip Kitcher, *Moral Progress* (New York: Oxford University Press, 2021).

20. On "ideal theory," see, for example, Charles Mills, "Ideal Theory as Ideology," in *Hypatia* 20, no. 3 (2005), 165–184. For a summary of the discussion on "ideal theory," see Laura Valentini, "Ideal vs. Non-Ideal Theory: A Conceptual Map," *Philosophy Compass* 7, no. 9 (2012), 654–664.

21. As has become customary, I capitalize Critical Theory when referring to the Critical Theory of the Frankfurt School; I drop the capital letters when referring to critical theories in the broader sense or in the plural.

22. On one such controversy, see Amy Allen and Rahel Jaeggi, "Progress, Normativity, and the Dynamics of Social Change: An Exchange between Rahel Jaeggi and Amy Allen," in *Graduate Faculty Philosophy Journal* 37, no. 2 (2016), 225–251, 226.

23. Rahel Jaeggi, trans. Ciaran Cronin, *Critique of Forms of Life* (Cambridge, MA: Harvard University Press, 2018).

Introduction

Epigraph: Theodor W. Adorno, trans. Anne G. Mitchell and Wesley V. Blomster, *Philosophy of Modern Music* (Minneapolis: University of Minnesota Press, 2006), xii; translation modified.

1. To temper any undue skepticism toward progress, it is worth noting that the developments I have just listed (with regional variations) were achieved relatively recently, many of them within living memory. Women were constitutionally guaranteed the right to vote in the United States in 1920, and in the country of my birth, Switzerland, only from the mid-1970s; in Germany, the right to a nonviolent upbringing has been enshrined in law only since 2000; §377A of the Singaporean penal code, which prohibited consensual sex between men as an act of "gross indecency," was repealed as recently as 2023. Homosexuality was classified as a disorder in the WHO's ICD-9 catalog until 1992.

2. Johann Nepomuk Nestroy, "Der Schützling: Posse mit Gesang in vier Akten," in Nestroy, *Sämtliche Werke: Historisch kritische Ausgabe*, Vol. 24: Stücke II, eds. John R. P. MacKenzie and Jürgen Hein (Vienna: Deuticke, 2000), 7–107, 91.

3. Peter Wagner, *Fortschritt: Zur Erneuerung einer Idee* (Frankfurt am Main: Campus, 2018), 28.

4. See Reinhart Koselleck, "'Progress' and 'Decline': An Appendix to the History of Two Concepts," in Koselleck, trans. Todd Samuel Presner, *The Practice of Conceptual History: Timing History, Spacing Concepts* (Stanford: Stanford University Press, 2002), 218–235. See also some of Koselleck's other essays collected in *Begriffsgeschichten: Studien zur Semantik und Pragmatik der politischen und sozialen Sprache* (Frankfurt am Main: Suhrkamp, 2006): "Sprachwandel und Ereignisgeschichte": 32–55, 45–48; "Die Geschichte der Begriffe und Begriffe der Geschichte": 56–77, 66–70; "Die Verzeitlichung der Begriffe": 77–85.

5. For a critique of process concepts, see Wolfgang Knöbl, *Die Soziologie vor der Geschichte: Zur Kritik der Sozialtheorie* (Berlin: Suhrkamp, 2022), 9–18.

6. See Wendy Brown, *Politics Out of History* (Princeton: Princeton University Press, 2001), 3.

7. Koselleck, "'Progress' and 'Decline,'" 225.

8. Koselleck, "'Progress' and 'Decline,'" 225. The reference to "savages," evidently still unproblematic in 1980, but also its pairing with "overseas colonization," gives us a first indication of how the idea of progress was entangled in colonialism from the outset.

9. Steven Lukes, "Das Ende des Fortschritts? Vom Sinn der Fortschrittsidee," POLAR 9 (2010), 7–13, 8 (emphasis added).

10. The theory of the development of the forces of production and its effect on the relations of production systematically spells out this assumed interconnection and gives it a materialist complexion. And *The Communist Manifesto* is also a manifesto for progress. Marx and Engels explain how "all that is solid melts into air" through the dynamic of industrialization and how, through the unleashed mastery of nature, social power relations become fluid and press for change. See Karl Marx and Friedrich Engels, *The Communist Manifesto* (London: Verso, 2012), 38.

11. See Koselleck, "'Progress' and 'Decline,'" 219. Koselleck's example of the father allowing his youngest son to sit with the adults at the dinner table despite not yet having been confirmed shows that progressive measures can be implemented without the reasons being understood.

12. G. W. F. Hegel, trans. H. B. Nisbet, *Lectures on the Philosophy of World History* (Cambridge, UK: Cambridge University Press, 1980), 83.

13. Koselleck, "'Progress' and 'Decline,'" 219.

14. This awareness of time resonates even in the blithe confidence expressed by protestors in 1968 that they stood as "progressive forces" on the right side of history. The contrast with the self-perception of today's protest movements is striking.

15. Anne Robert Jacques Turgot, "Tableau philosophique des progrès successifs de l'esprit humain," in *Oeuvres de Turgot et documents le concernant, Vol. 1*, ed. Gustave Schelle (Paris: F. Alcan, 1913), 215.

16. Walter Benjamin, trans. Harry Zohn, "Theses on the Philosophy of History," in Benjamin, *Illuminations* (London: Pimlico, 1999), 245–255, 251.

17. John Dewey, "Progress," *International Journal of Ethics* 26, no. 3 (1916): 311–322, 311.

18. Benjamin, "Theses on the Philosophy of History," 250. For a helpful discussion of this constellation in Benjamin, see Andrea Messner, "Über den Begriff des Fortschritts bei Walter Benjamin" (unpublished Masters' thesis, Berlin, 2018).

19. Sebastian Conrad and Jürgen Osterhammel, eds., *An Emerging Modern World, 1750–1870* (Cambridge, MA: Belknap Press of Harvard University Press, 2018), 24.

20. See Terry Pinkard, "Hegel's False Start: Non-Europeans as Failed Europeans," in Pinkard, *Does History Make Sense? Hegel on the Historical Shapes of Justice* (Cambridge, MA: Harvard University Press, 2017), 50–67.

21. Stuart Hall, "The West and the Rest: Discourse and Power," in *Essential Essays, Vol. 2: Identity and Diaspora,* ed. David Morley (Durham: Duke University Press, 2018), 141–184.

22. Dipesh Chakrabarty, *Provincializing Europe: Postcolonial Thought and Historical Difference* (Princeton: Princeton University Press, 2000), 8.

23. Katharina Döbler offers readers an informed literary insight into the real history of German colonialism in her novel, *Dein ist das Reich* (Berlin: Claassen, 2021).

24. Ashis Nandy, "Two Hundred Years of Silence," *Le Monde Diplomatique,* October 2015, https://mondediplo.com/2015/10/14supp.

25. Thomas McCarthy, *Race, Empire, and the Idea of Human Development* (Cambridge, UK: Cambridge University Press, 2009), 166.

26. See Serene J. Khader, *Decolonizing Universalism: A Transnational Feminist Ethic* (New York: Oxford University Press, 2019), who criticizes such imperialist proselytizing from a feminist perspective.

27. Conrad and Osterhammel, *An Emerging Modern World*, 17.

28. Adorno's relationship to the philosophy of history is complex: he regards it as both indispensable and problematic. See Isette Schuhmacher, "Fortschritt nach Adorno," unpublished Masters' thesis, Humboldt University, Berlin, 2017. On Adorno's philosophy of history, see also Rahel Jaeggi and Isette Schuhmacher, "Adorno's Negative Philosophy of History," in *The Oxford Handbook of Adorno,* eds. Martin Shuster and Henry Pickford (forthcoming from Oxford University Press).

29. This risk is pointed out by Robin Celikates, "Moralischer Fortschritt, soziale Kämpfe und Emanzipationsblockaden. Elemente einer Kri-

tischen Theorie der Politik," in *Kritische Theorie der Politik*, eds. Ulf Bohmann and Paul Sörensen (Berlin: Suhrkamp, 2019), 397–425.

30. Michel Foucault, trans. C. Gordon, "Prison Talk," in Foucault, *Power/ Knowledge: Selected Interviews and Other Writings, 1972–1977* (New York: Vintage, 1980), 37–54, 49–50.

31. For an early example of this point, see Hinrich Fink-Eitel, *Die Philosophie und die Wilden: Über die Bedeutung des Fremden für die europäische Geistesgeschichte* (Hamburg: Junius, 1994). As noted earlier, Koselleck clearly found it unproblematic to speak of "savages." The discomfort we involuntarily feel when reading such language today is a sign of at least some progress in perception.

32. See Philippe Ariès, *Centuries of Childhood: A Social History of Family Life* (New York: Vintage/Ebury, 1962); on the transformation of family relations and the emergence of a female "inner space," see Gisela Bock, trans. Allison Brown, *Women in European History* (Oxford: Blackwell, 2002).

33. The classic study is Jürgen Habermas, trans. T. Burger, *The Structural Transformation of the Public Sphere* (Cambridge, MA: Harvard University Press, 1991).

34. Dietmar Dath and Barbara Kirchner are among the few authors writing today who are explicitly interested in social progress in an integrative sense. They define social progress as "the increase in freedom, participation, and subsistence for ever more people, associated with gains in information and productivity, and the simultaneous elimination of exclusion, oppression, and exploitation." See Dietmar Dath and Barbara Kirchner, *Der Implex: Sozialer Fortschritt: Geschichte und Idee* (Berlin: Suhrkamp, 2012). Hauke Brunkhorst also emphasizes a materialist side in his *Critical Theory of Legal Revolutions: Evolutionary Perspectives* (New York: Bloomsbury, 2014).

35. Christian Schmidt, unpublished Ms., Berlin, 2022.

36. In this sense, Marx writes in *The German Ideology*: "In history up to the present it is certainly an empirical fact that separate individuals have, with the broadening of their activity into world-historical activity, become more and more enslaved under a power alien to them (a pressure which they have conceived of as a dirty trick on the part of the so-called universal spirit, etc.), a power which has become more and more enormous and, in the last instance, turns out to be the *world market*." Karl Marx and Frederick Engels, *The German Ideology: Part*

One, ed. Christopher John Arthur (New York: International Publishing, 1970), 55.

37. Bhambra writes: "The modern social, or modernity, is seen to be constituted as the outcome of endogenous processes of European history. These include the processes of economic and political change associated with the Industrial and French revolutions and underpinned by the cultural changes brought about by the Renaissance, the Reformation, and the Scientific Revolution. The rest of the world is presented as outside these world-historical processes, and furthermore colonial connections are seen as insignificant to their development. Such an understanding conflates Europe with modernity and renders the process of becoming modern, at least in the first instance, one of endogenous European development." Gurminder K. Bhambra, "Decolonizing Critical Theory? Epistemological Justice, Progress, Reparations," *Critical Times* 4, no. 1 (2021), 73–80, 79.

38. Stuart Hall, "Europe's Other Self," *Marxism Today,* August 1991, 18–19, 18.

39. Yves Winter, "Formally Decolonized but Still Neocolonial?," *Political Theory* 46 (5) 2018, 785–790.

40. Koselleck, "'Progress' and 'Decline,'" 228.

41. I borrow this concept from Isette Schuhmacher, who identifies Adorno's idea of progress as "fractured dialectics" (*brüchige Dialektik*). See Schuhmacher, "Fortschritt nach Adorno."

42. I thank Friedrich Weissbach for forcing me to clarify this point through his interview questions: "Rahel Jaeggi: 'Fortschritt ist weder Fakt noch Ideal.' Rahel Jaeggi im Interview mit Friedrich Weissbach," in *Philosophie Magazin,* June 22, 2022, https://www.philomag.de/artikel/rahel-jaeggi-fortschritt-ist-weder-fakt-noch-ideal.

43. On this distinction with reference to Dewey and Hegel, see Rahel Jaeggi, trans. Ciaran Cronin, *Critique of Forms of Life* (Cambridge MA: Harvard University Press, 2018), 133–172.

44. Edward Said, *Orientalism* (London: Penguin, 2019). See also Jürgen Osterhammel and Jan C. Jansen, *Kolonialismus: Geschichte, Formen, Folgen* (Munich: C. H. Beck, 1995).

45. See Peter Singer, *The Expanding Circle: Ethics, Evolution, and Moral Progress* (Princeton: Princeton University Press, 1981).

1. What Is Progress?

Epigraph: Theodor W. Adorno, trans. Henry W. Pickford, "Progress," in *Critical Models: Interventions and Catchwords* (New York: Columbia University Press, 2005), 143–160, 143.

1. Slavery has been abolished as a recognized social institution even if, yes, modern forms of slavery persist in the form of forced prostitution, human trafficking, the recruitment of child soldiers, and the US prison system. On this last point, see Michelle Alexander, *The New Jim Crow: Mass Incarceration in the Age of Colorblindness* (New York: New Press, 2010). The renowned slavery scholar Kevin Bales estimates that at least twenty-seven million people live in conditions of enslavement at the dawn of the twenty-first century. See Kevin Bales, *Disposable People: New Slavery in the Global Economy* (Berkeley: University of California Press, 2008), 8. As correct as it may be to speak of "slavery" here, we should not erase the differences between slavery as a legally and ethically recognized institution and "modern slavery," which operates under the cover of debt bondage or criminal justice systems precisely because it has been outlawed everywhere.

2. Rape in marriage was not explicitly permitted before, of course. By definition, there was no spousal rape because rape (in Germany) was defined as "extramarital" until 1997. In Germany, a child's right to a "nonviolent upbringing" has been guaranteed by law only since 2001.

3. See, among others, Elizabeth Anderson, "The Social Epistemology of Morality: Learning from the Forgotten History of the Abolition of Slavery," in *The Epistemic Life of Groups: Essays in the Epistemology of Collectives,* eds. Miranda Frikker and Michael Brady (Oxford: Oxford University Press, 2016), 75–94; Elizabeth Anderson, "Social Movements, Experiments in Living, and Moral Progress: Case Studies from Britain's Abolition of Slavery," Lindley Lecture for 2014, University of Kansas, Lawrence, KS, February 11, 2014, 2, text available at https://hdl.handle.net/1808/14787; Kwame Antony Appiah, *The Honor Code: How Moral Revolutions Happen* (London: W. W. Norton, 2011); Michelle Moody-Adams, "The Idea of Moral Progress," *Metaphilosophy* 30, no. 3 (1999): 168–185; Philip Kitcher, *The Ethical Project* (Cambridge, MA: Harvard University Press, 2011).

4. Theodor W. Adorno, trans. Henry W. Pickford, "Progress," in *Critical Models: Interventions and Catchwords* (New York: Columbia University Press, 2005), 143.

5. Legal codification can be understood as the expression and result of social change, a transformed ethical life, or shifts in forms of life as webs of practices and institutions. Yet legal codification in turn feeds into such change, meaning that the influence runs both ways. This reciprocal influence is an important point that I cannot expand on here.

6. For an astonishingly clear example of the latter from a reputable German news source, see Sabine Rückert, "Das Schlafzimmer als gefährlicher Ort," in *Zeit Online*, June 30, 2016, https://www.zeit.de /2016/28/sexualstrafrecht-verschaerfung-kritik.

7. Georg Henrik von Wright, "Progress: Fact and Fiction," in *The Idea of Progress*, ed. Arnold Burgen (Berlin: De Gruyter, 1997), 1–18, 1.

8. Gereon Wolters, "The Idea of Progress in Evolutionary Biology: Philosophical Considerations," in *The Idea of Progress*, ed. Arnold Burgen (Berlin: De Gruyter, 1997), 201–218, 201.

9. On "thick concepts," see Bernard Williams, *Ethics and the Limits of Philosophy* (Cambridge, MA: Harvard University Press, 1985), 158–163. On the debate on the metaethical consequences of assuming value-laden facts, see Hilary Putnam, "Werte und Normen," in *Die Öffentlichkeit der Vernunft und die Vernunft der Öffentlichkeit: Festschrift für Jürgen Habermas*, eds. Klaus Günther and Lutz Wingert (Frankfurt am Main: Suhrkamp, 2001), 280–313. On the interpenetration of analytical and descriptive elements in the process of immanent critique, see Rahel Jaeggi, "Was ist Ideologiekritik?" in *Was ist Kritik?*, eds. Rahel Jaeggi and Tilo Wesche (Frankfurt am Main: Suhrkamp, 2009), 266–298, 281–283, and Rahel Jaeggi and Robin Celikates, *Einführung in die Sozialphilosophie* (Munich: C. H. Beck, 2017), 17–20.

10. From this perspective, a norm-free, neutral description of the social world to which evaluation is then added is implausible. Interestingly, a number of otherwise very different philosophical positions converge in their efforts to break the dominance of an empiricist worldview based on the assumption of a normatively neutral world. See Alice Crary, *Inside Ethics: On the Demands of Moral Thought* (Cambridge, MA: Harvard University Press, 2016), esp. ch. 1: "Outside Ethics: Tracing a Trend in Contemporary Moral Philosophy," 10–35. On the convergence of these positions with anti-positivism see also Crary, "The

Methodological is the Political: What's the Matter with 'Analytic Feminism'?" *Radical Philosophy* 202 (2018): 47–60.

11. Such a deontologization of progress is pursued—albeit for different reasons and with different perspectives—by Rainer Forst, "The Justification of Progress and the Progress of Justification," in *Justification and Emancipation: The Political Philosophy of Rainer Forst*, eds. Amy Allen and Eduardo Mendieta (University Park: Pennsylvania State University Press, 2019), 17–37, and Christian Thies, "Kants Geschichtsphilosophie aus heutiger Sicht," in *Kant, L'Anthropologie et L'Histoire*, eds. Olivier Ayard and Françoise Lartillot (Paris, l'Harmattan, 2011), 35–49.

12. Forst, "Justification of Progress and the Progress of Justification," 20.

13. The same problem was addressed in Korea by cooking soup, highlighting that there can be functionally equivalent solutions to the same problem. I thank Josefine Berkholz for this reference.

14. See Kitcher, *The Ethical Project*, and Kitcher, *Moral Progress* (New York: Oxford University Press, 2021), 25.

15. Antonio Machado, "CXXXVI Proverbios y cantares," in Machado, trans. W. Barnstone, *Border of a Dream: Selected Poems of Antonio Machado* (Port Townsend, WA: Copper Canyon, 2013), 281. In the original: "Caminante, no hay camino / se hace camino al andar. / Al andar se hace el camino."

16. Terry Pinkard, *Does History Make Sense? Hegel on the Historical Shape of Justice* (Cambridge, MA: Harvard University Press, 2017), 2.

17. Frederick Neuhouser, "Desire, Recognition, and the Relation between Bondsman and Lord," in *The Blackwell Guide to Hegel's Phenomenology of Spirit*, ed. Kenneth R. Westphal (Oxford: Wiley-Blackwell, 2009), 39.

18. John Dewey, "Democracy and Education," in *The Middle Works of John Dewey, Vol. 9*, ed. Jo Ann Boydston (Carbondale, IL: Southern Illinois University Press, 2008), 62. See Rahel Jaeggi, trans. Ciaran Cronin, *Critique of Forms of Life* (Cambridge, MA: Harvard University Press, 2018), 244–245.

19. The debate sparked by Thomas S. Kuhn, *The Structure of Scientific Revolutions* (Chicago: University of Chicago Press, 1962); Imre Lakatos, "Falsification and the Methodology of Scientific Research Programmes," in *Criticism and the Growth of Knowledge: Proceedings of the International Colloquium in the Philosophy of Science*, eds.

Imre Lakatos and Alan Musgrave (Cambridge, UK: Cambridge University Press, 1970), 91–196; and Paul Feyerabend, *Against Method* (London: New Left Books, 1975), is of lasting significance for the theory of science. On Laudan's position, see Larry Laudan, *Progress and Its Problems: Towards a Theory of Scientific Growth* (Berkeley: University of California Press, 1977).

20. Laudan, *Progress and its Problems*, 5–6.

21. Laudan, *Progress and its Problems*, 6.

22. I borrow the phrase from Max Horkheimer and Theodor W. Adorno, who used it in a very different context and with different implications. Max Horkheimer and Theodor W. Adorno, trans. E. Jephcott, *Dialectic of Enlightenment* (Stanford: Stanford University Press, 2002), xi.

23. Laudan, *Progress and its Problems*, 5.

24. See Kitcher, *The Ethical Project*, 139, 210, 239.

25. Theodor W. Adorno, trans. R. Livingstone, *Problems of Moral Philosophy* (Stanford: Stanford University Press, 2000), 175.

26. How exactly the temporality and historicity of the transformation process in question (and hence also the historicity of the good) are understood will then prove crucial. In this respect, we will see later on, in Chapters 4 and 5, how a dialectical-pragmatic position of progressive change as a process of enrichment (such as the one offered here) differs from a naturalist-pragmatic position (such as Kitcher's). We will also see that the corresponding problem-solving processes must be conceived in the mode of determinate negation, as processes of dialectical enrichment, if they are to be at all meaningful in normative terms.

27. Laudan, *Progress and its Problems*, 5.

28. Walter Benjamin, trans. Harry Zohn, "Theses on the Philosophy of History," in Benjamin, *Illuminations* (London: Pimlico, 1999), 245–255, 252.

29. For a more detailed elaboration of a pragmatically inspired conception of learning see Jaeggi, *Critique of Forms of Life*, esp. Chapter 7.1, 221–226. On the theorem of blockages to learning see *Critique of Forms of Life*, Chapter 7.3, 230–233.

30. I closely align "having an experience" with "learning" here as, in my view, experience should not be conceived as a passive affair. In addition, learning is problem-driven and not a purely cognitive process. Herein lies a possible difference from Christoph Menke, *Theorie der Befreiung* (Berlin: Suhrkamp, 2022).

31. On the distinction between normative and normativist, see Michael Theunissen, "Möglichkeiten des Philosophierens heute," in Theunissen, *Negative Theologie der Zeit* (Frankfurt am Main: Suhrkamp, 1991): 13–36, 31.

32. Realistically, it is doubtful whether a historical condition brought about in this way could be sustained without at least subsequently undergoing such a development. The fact that in Germany, victory over National Socialism did indeed fall from the sky, in a manner of speaking, and was not the result of an internal uprising is instructive in this regard. In this case, the actual learning process, and with it the progressive overcoming of societal attitudes, practices, and institutions deeply shaped by the Nazi regime and its antidemocratic antecedents, had to be carried out retroactively. Here there was no alternative; the preconditions for such a development first had to be imposed from without. Other attempts to organize social transformation processes, for instance through democratization, have proven to be more likely to succeed when they can build on endogenous processes, developments, and movements.

33. In speaking positively here about learning or experience and negatively about blockages to learning and systematic failures to learn, I obviously do not have in mind the "unlearning" called for in debates about decolonization. See, for example, Madina V. Tlostanova and Walter Mignolo, *Learning to Unlearn: Decolonial Reflections from Eurasia and the Americas* (Columbus: Ohio State University Press, 2012), where it is a question of unlearning ingrained colonial perspectives that warp and limit experience. Learning, as I understand it here, would encompass just such a form of unlearning. Put differently, the unlearning process demanded by Mignolo is a process for dismantling epistemic blockages as part of a successful experiential learning process.

34. Theodor W. Adorno, trans. E. B. Ashton, *Negative Dialectics* (London: Routledge, 1973), 13.

35. I thank Al Prescott-Couch for drawing my attention to this parallel.

2. Reform or Revolution: Continuity or Discontinuity of Progress

Epigraph: Karl Marx, "Letters from the Deutsch-Französische Jahrbücher," in *Marx and Engels Collected Works*, Vol. 3 (London: Lawrence & Wishart, 1974), 144; translation modified.

1. See Kwame Antony Appiah, *The Honor Code: How Moral Revolutions Happen* (New York: W. W. Norton, 2010).
2. At this point, I am not concerned with distinguishing between moral and social perspectives, which is why I will refer indiscriminately, and depending on the terminology used by the authors discussed, to moral, social, or normative change.
3. This chapter has benefited from Kristina Lepold's commentary and suggestions.
4. See Peter Singer, *The Expanding Circle: Ethics, Evolution, and Moral Progress* (Princeton: Princeton University Press, 1981).
5. Michael Walzer, *Interpretation and Social Criticism* (Cambridge, MA: Harvard University Press, 1987), 27.
6. This is how Philip Kitcher describes the "expanding the circle" view (which he views very critically). See Philip Kitcher, *The Ethical Project* (Cambridge, MA: Harvard University Press, 2011), 214.
7. Henry Richardson calls this process the "correction of prior errors," as opposed to real "moral innovations." See Henry Richardson, *Articulating the Moral Community: Toward a Constructive Ethical Pragmatism* (New York: Oxford University Press, 2018), 19.
8. Richard Rorty is among the most prominent defenders of this position: "[Moral] progress should not be conceived of as the convergence of human opinion to Moral Truth or as the onset of greater rationality, but rather as an increase in our ability to see more and more differences among people as morally irrelevant." Richard Rorty, *Truth and Progress: Philosophical Papers* (Cambridge, UK: Cambridge University Press, 1991), 11. Typically, an important role in such a development is played by *empathy*, the ability to put oneself in someone else's shoes. Rorty made much of the power of literature to stimulate the imagination, allowing us to empathize with others as sentient and suffering beings.
9. Rorty, *Truth and Progress*, 11.
10. Hazel Rosenstrauch, *Aus Nachbarn wurden Juden: Ausgrenzung und Selbstbehauptung 1933–1942* (Berlin: Transit, 1988).
11. I will not presume to adjudicate whether this is an incidental or a systematically necessary characteristic of the approaches grouped together here—that is, whether there is a variant of the expanding circle theory that can better address the contentious aspects of the change.
12. For criticism of such processes of integration and normalization, see for example the discussion of "marriage equality," by which queers

living in long-term monogamous relationships are integrated into mainstream society while others are exiled to their different forms of life precisely through the presumption that "they are like us."

13. Allen Buchanan and Russell Powell list a number of modes of progressive change that do not align with the type of expansion. Allen Buchanan and Russell Powell, "Toward a Naturalistic Theory of Moral Progress," *Ethics* 126, no. 4 (2016): 983–1014.

14. Kitcher, *Ethical Project*, 215.

15. What is ultimately overcome here is the idea of retribution. This stands at odds with our moral universe, especially in the form in which it also applies to members of the family identified with the criminal. For example, the death of a sister can be avenged with the death of another sister (not necessarily even the killer's).

16. Kitcher, *Ethical Project*, 215.

17. See Peter Singer, *Practical Ethics*, Cambridge 1980, 48–70.

18. Jürgen Habermas, "Über den doppelten Boden des demokratischen Rechtsstaates," in Habermas, *Eine Art Schadensabwicklung: Kleine Politische Schriften VI* (Frankfurt am Main: Suhrkamp, 1987), 18–23, 19.

19. For an example of this view, see Axel Honneth, "Rejoinder," *Critical Horizons* 16, no. 2 (2015), 204–226, 211.

20. See Axel Honneth, trans. Joseph Ganahl, *Freedom's Right: The Social Foundations of Democratic Right* (Cambridge, UK: Polity, 2014).

21. For a theory of the emergence of new moral norms in the sense of articulation, see Matt Congdon, *Moral Articulation: On the Development of New Moral Concepts* (Oxford: Oxford University Press, 2023).

22. See the last chapter in Honneth, *Freedom's Right*; in addition, Honneth is sometimes criticized for downplaying the contentious nature of social struggles due to their normative predetermination; see Robin Celikates and Georg Bertram, "Nicht versöhnt: Wo bleibt der Kampf im 'Kampf um Anerkennung'?," in *Socialité et reconnaissance: Grammaires de l'humain*, eds. Georg W. Bertram et al. (Paris 2017), 213–228.

23. Axel Honneth, "Die Normativität der Sittlichkeit: Hegels Lehre als Alternative zur Ethik Kants," *Deutsche Zeitschrift für Philosophie* 62, no. 5 (2014): 787–800.

24. See Honneth, "Rejoinder," 210. To be sure, Honneth distinguishes here between institutional processes of change, which can indeed assume a revolutionary character, and transformations of the normative framework.

25. See Walter Benjamin, trans. H. Zohn, "Theses on the Philosophy of History," in Benjamin, *Illuminations* (London: Pimlico, 1999), 245–255, 261.

26. William Sewell thus points out that even the gruesome revolutionary practice of impaling severed heads on pikes had a traditional background. William H. Sewell Jr., "Historical Events as Transformations of Structures: Inventing Revolution at the Bastille," *Theory and Society* 25, no. 6 (1996): 841–881, 869.

27. This conception of legitimacy is emphasized in Karl Griewank, *Der neuzeitliche Revolutionsbegriff: Entstehung und Entwicklung* (Hamburg: Europäische Verlagsanstalt, 1992).

28. This theory is negatively mirrored in the above-mentioned fear of some queer theorists that "marriage equality" introduces heteronormative principles into queer lifestyles and leads to new exclusions.

29. That is one of the reasons why such questions are so fiercely and violently contested in the age of regression, even though from a liberal standpoint (and hence a standpoint that valorizes individual freedom of choice) there seems to be nothing more to it than an expansion of options.

30. Emmanuel Joseph Sieyès, trans. M. Blondel, *What Is the Third Estate?* (Ann Arbor MI: University of Michigan Press, 1964), 51.

31. Jacques Rancière, trans. J. Rose, *Disagreement: Politics and Philosophy* (Minneapolis: University of Minnesota Press, 1999), 77.

32. See Karl Marx, trans. C. J. Arthur, *The German Ideology: Part One* (New York, 1970), 57.

33. Alex Demirovic highlights the questionable nature of this alternative today, arguing instead for the concept of transformation. See Demirovic, "Reform, Revolution, Transformation," *Journal für Entwicklungspolitik* XXVIII (2012): 16–43.

34. The phrase "non-reformist reform" was coined by André Gorz and is used today by various Leftist movements. See Mark Engler and Paul Engler, "Die nicht-reformistischen Reformen von André Gorz," *Jacobin.de,* August 6, 2021, https://jacobin.de/artikel/andre-gorz-nich treformistischen-reformen-neue-linke-ivan-illich-reform-revolution/.

3. In Context: Moral Progress and Social Change

Epigraph: Karl Marx and Friedrich Engels, trans. Helen Macfarlane, *The Communist Manifesto* (New York: Signet Classics, 2011), 90; translation modified.

1. Elizabeth Anderson, "The Social Epistemology of Morality: Learning from the Forgotten History of the Abolition of Slavery," in Miranda Fricker and Michael Brady, eds., *The Epistemic Life of Groups: Essays in Collective Epistemology* (Oxford 2016), 75–94, 76.
2. Karl Marx, trans. D. Fernbach, *Capital: A Critique of Political Economy: Volume III* (London 1992), 911; translation modified.
3. In context, Marx refers to private ownership of human beings as a broad phenomenon that can encompass not only slavery but also various forms of feudal vassalage.
4. See the definitional entry for "Abgeschmackt. Schal. Fade." ("Tasteless. Insipid. Stale.") in Johann August Eberhard, *Synonymisches Handwörterbuch der deutschen Sprache,* ed. Otto Lyon, seventeenth edition (Leipzig: Grieben, 1910), which instructs that something is tasteless, *abgeschmackt,* if it has "lost its natural, pleasant taste." The entry further clarifies: "In a figurative sense, *tasteless* means what is *lacking* in taste or even goes *against* taste and offends finer sensibilities, e.g., a tasteless headdress." *Tasteless,* "primarily denotes the *aberrant taste* that confronts us in speech, clothing, art, etc. It expresses greater disapprobation than the word *geschmacklos.*" In the following entry, he describes the word as conveying "the adverse impression made on our sensibility by everything that flagrantly offends reason." Entry (in German) accessible at https://www.textlog.de/eberhard/synonyme/abgeschmackt-schal-fade.
5. The fact that slavery still exists, and was even more widespread in Marx's lifetime, is another matter. The British abolished slavery in the West Indies in 1838, while the Thirteenth Amendment banning slavery in the United States dates from 1865. E. Benjamin Skinner reports on the perpetuation of modern forms of slavery in *A Crime So Monstrous: Face-to-Face with Modern-Day Slavery* (New York: Free Press, 2008). See also Kevin Bales, *Disposable People: New Slavery in the Global Economy,* revised edition (Berkeley: University of California Press, 2012). Anderson is nonetheless right to argue: "Although *de facto* slavery persists in many areas of the world, virtually no one is willing to publicly defend it." Elizabeth Anderson, "Social Movements, Experiments in Living, and Moral Progress: Case Studies from Britain's Abolition of Slavery," Lindley Lecture for 2014, University of Kansas, Lawrence, KS, February 11, 2014, 2. Text available at https://hdl.handle.net/1808/14787.
6. On the term "proto-values," see Georg Lohmann, "Zwei Konzeptionen von Gerechtigkeit in Marx' Kapitalismuskritik," in *Ethik und*

Marx: Moralkritik und normative Grundlagen der Marxschen Theorie, eds. Georg Lohmann and Emil Angehrn (Königstein: Hain bei Athenaum, 1986), 174–194, 175.

7. Egon Flaig, *Weltgeschichte der Sklaverei* (Munich 2018). With his thesis of the slave's "social death," Orlando Patterson has shown that slavery involves a specific relationship compared to other historical forms of human bondage. See Orlando Patterson, *Slavery and Social Death: A Comparative Study* (Cambridge MA 1982).

8. Anderson, "Social Movements, Experiments in Living, and Moral Progress," 1– 3.

9. Given Christianity's history of violence, including under colonialism, this is by no means to say that being a Christian has in itself ever prevented anyone from committing acts of cruelty. The tension I want to highlight here is not that between Christian charity and cruelty but between painstaking self-scrutiny and a blatant disregard for what is obvious (to us).

10. This was a transition that Anderson's captain—his name was John Newton—experienced in person, becoming a priest and later an abolitionist. This personal conversion does not interest me here, however.

11. Alasdair MacIntyre, "Epistemological Crisis, Dramatic Narrative, and the Philosophy of Science," in *The Monist* 60, no. 4 (1997), 453–472.

12. On this ambiguous image from gestalt psychology, see Ludwig Wittgenstein, trans. G. Anscombe, *Philosophical Investigations* (Chichester 2009), 165–175.

13. Friedrich Schiller, trans. R. Snell, *On the Aesthetic Education of Man* (Mineola NY 2004).

14. Richard Rorty, *Truth and Progress: Philosophical Papers* (Cambridge 1991), 176.

15. G.W.F. Hegel, trans. H.B. Nisbet, *Lectures on the Philosophy of World History* (Cambridge 1975), 83

16. Karl Marx and Friedrich Engels, *The German Ideology,* ed. C. J. Arthur (New York 1970), 47.

17. Anderson, "The Social Epistemology of Morality," 76.

18. These critical objections are too well known to need rehashing here. See Jürgen Habermas, *Zur Rekonstruktion des Historischen Materialismus* (Frankfurt am Main: 1976). See also, from an entirely different perspective, Louis Althusser, "Contradiction and Overdetermination," in Althusser, trans. B. Brewster, *For Marx* (London 2005), 87–128.

Jorge Larrain, *A Reconstruction of Historical Materialism* (London 1986) provides a good overview of the discussion.

19. At this point I have no interest in divining what the "real Marx" might have meant or in deciding what the most fruitful reading of Marx might be—there is clearly a wide range of useful interpretations in relation to the questions arising here that oppose such simplistic approaches with support from Marx himself.

20. When the German Civil Code took effect on January 1, 1900, it stipulated in § 1354: "The husband has the right to decide all matters relating to matrimonial life." In questions of household management and childrearing, too, the husband had the final say. He was legally entitled to manage and enjoy the proceeds from his wife's estate. In other words, if a woman entered the marriage with money of her own, her husband alone could dispose of it and draw income from her assets. This law essentially remained in force until March 31, 1953. It was not until 1957 that a new legal regime governing matrimonial property, the so-called community of accrued gains (*Zugewinngemeinschaft*), came into force with the passage of the Equal Rights Act. In 1961 the Family Law Amendment Act brought changes to the legal relationship between parents and children as well as to marriage and divorce law. I thank Christina Clemm for providing information and advice on this topic.

21. This is how Otto von Gierke justified his rejection of a marriage law reform in 1920. See Eva Marie von Münch, "Hausfrauen-Ehe abgeschafft," *Die Zeit* 43 (1976), http://www.zeit.de/1976/43/hausfrauen-ehe-abgeschafft.

22. See Sabine Rückert, "Das Schlafzimmer als gefährlicher Ort," *Die Zeit* 28 (2016), https://www.zeit.de/2016/28/sexualstrafrechtverschaerfung-kritik.

23. It is no coincidence that rape is a kind of domination and subjugation that is commonplace in war and has characterized feudal power relations. The decisive question here is which practice we are actually talking about. The term "sexualized violence" first allows a certain relationship to be recognized *as* one of violence, and has thus made a key contribution to reinterpreting this social practice. On the persistence of violence against women, but also on the way the law continues to deny and trivialize it—even after its delegitimization—see Christina Clemm, *Akteneinsicht* (Munich 2020), and Patrícia Melo, *Gestapelte Frauen* (Zürich 2021).

24. The term *poisonous pedagogy* was coined by Katharina Rutschky and taken up by Alice Miller. See Rutschky, ed., *Schwarze Pädagogik: Quellen zur Naturgeschichte der bürgerlichen Erziehung* (Berlin: Ullstein, 1977).

25. Michael Haneke paints an ingenious portrait of this imaginative world in his film *The White Ribbon*.

26. The backlash in the 1950s, when domesticity and female devotion were celebrated propagandistically in films, advertisements, and other media, can be understood against this background.

27. Setting historical inaccuracies to one side, this is the least that could be said in criticism of this sepia-tinged account. Solely the fact that sexual relations between master and maid were more the rule than the exception (as presented here), and were far from consensual, reciprocal, and loving, makes the euphemistic nature of the television series clear. In reality, most of the young women in question were probably raped without recourse to legal redress.

28. The social impact of the typewriter and the concomitant emergence of a female white-collar culture have been captured many times in literature. Particularly illuminating in this regard are the novels of Irmgard Keun, which depict the lives of female office workers in the Weimar Republic between emancipation and the expectation of marriage. See, for example, Irmgard Keun, trans. Kathie von Ankum, *The Artificial Silk Girl* [1932] (New York: Other Press, 2002). The same milieu was given sociological treatment in Siegfried Kracauer's early study *The Salaried Masses: Duty and Distraction in Weimar Germany* [1930], trans. Quintin Hoare (London: Verso, 1998), and has recently been popularized in the television series *Babylon Berlin* (from 2017), based on the novels of Volker Kutscher.

29. On unintended consequences, see the classic text by Robert K. Merton, "The Unanticipated Consequences of Purposive Social Action," *American Sociological Review* 1.6 (1936), 894–904.

30. Kwame Anthony Appiah, *The Honor Code: How Moral Revolutions Happen* (New York: W. W. Norton, 2010), Chapter 3.

31. I owe this example to a conversation with Terry Pinkard.

32. On this point I owe a great deal to the instructive commentary of Anna Katharina Sodoma and Titus Stahl.

33. For more on contention over moral principles, see Anderson, "The Social Epistemology of Morality," 76.

34. On the separation of morality and ethical life implicitly criticized here, see Rahel Jaeggi, trans. Ciaran Cronin, *Critique of Forms of Life* (Cambridge, MA: Harvard University Press, 2018), esp. the Introduction, 1–32, where I discuss this distinction using the example of violence in education and in relation to Habermas.

35. See G. W. F. Hegel, trans. H. B. Nisbet, *Elements of the Philosophy of Right* (Cambridge, UK: Cambridge University Press, 1991), Part Two: Morality, 133–186. On the relationship between morality and ethics, see Rüdiger Bubner, "Moralität und Sittlichkeit—die Herkunft eines Gegensatzes," and Jürgen Habermas, "Moralität und Sittlichkeit: Treffen Hegels Einwände gegen Kant auch auf die Diskursethik zu?," both in *Moralität und Sittlichkeit: Das Problem Hegels und die Diskursethik*, ed. Wolfgang Kuhlmann (Frankfurt am Main: Suhrkamp. 1986), 46–84, 16–37.

36. Anderson, "The Social Epistemology of Morality," 76.

37. Presumably, no moral discussion in recent decades has done more to improve the treatment of babies and toddlers than Daniel Stern's *Diary of a Baby*, which draws on the latest research findings to vividly depict the world experienced by newborn children. Daniel N. Stern, *Diary of a Baby: What Your Child Sees, Feels, and Experiences* (New York: Basic Books, 1992).

38. See Alice Crary, *Inside Ethics: On the Demands of Moral Thought* (Cambridge, MA: Harvard University Press, 2016).

39. Hence the close connection between early Critical Theory and epistemology.

40. See Theodor W. Adorno, trans. E. F. N. Jephcott, *Minima Moralia: Reflections from Damaged Life* (London: New Left Books, 1974), 27, 196.

41. Pascal, quoted in Louis Althusser, trans. G.M. Goshgarian, *On the Reproduction of Capitalism: Ideology and Ideological State Apparatuses* (London 2014), 186.

42. Anderson, "The Social Epistemology of Morality," 177.

43. Anderson, "The Social Epistemology of Morality," 177.

44. Philippa Foot, "Morality as a System of Hypothetical Imperatives," *The Philosophical Review* 81, no. 3 (1972), 305–316.

45. Anna Katarina Sodoma, "Functionalist Conceptions of Moral Progress and the Plurality of Ways of Life," in *Jahrbuch Praktische Philosophie in globaler Perspektive, Bd. 3: Moralischer Fortschritt*, eds. Michael

Reder et al. (Munich: Karl Alber, 2019): 50–72, 52. One objection to the functionalist approach could be that it is all too instrumentalist. In my view, however, the charge of instrumentalism is mitigated once one realizes that social cooperation is not an arbitrary goal. I do not decide on a whim if I will cooperate (in principle). Rather, the norms of coexistence make the fact of cooperation (and dependency) explicit—and as such malleable and negotiable. They do not create cooperation in the first place, and certainly not "from scratch." This reverses the starting point in relation to atomistic and contractualist conceptions: cooperation is the starting point; it is noncooperation that demands explanation.

46. See Johannes Rohbeck, *Geschichtsphilosophie zur Einführung* (Hamburg: Junius, 2015).

47. I developed this terminology in Part 1 of *Critique of Forms of Life*, esp. 55–84.

48. Burkhard Liebsch, "Lebensformen zwischen Widerstreit und Gewalt: Zur Topographie eines Forschungsfeldes im Jahr 2000," in *Lebensformen im Widerstreit: Integrations–und Identitätskonflikte in pluralen Gesellschaften,* eds. Burkhard Liebsch and Jürgen Straub (Frankfurt am Main: Campus, 2003), 13–44, 17.

49. Lutz Wingert, *Gemeinsinn und Moral: Grundzüge einer intersubjektivistischen Moralkonzeption* (Frankfurt am Main: 1993), 174.

50. The concept of forms of life is materialist and not culturalist in the sense that it emphasizes the interaction and interdependence of the different spheres and insists that forms of life have a material basis. That said, the concept also assumes that this basis is culturally and normatively shaped.

51. In this sense, social institutions are a comparatively "solid" aggregate state of practices, although there are also more "fluid" ones.

52. For a related understanding of social practices that takes a different view of their normative character, see Sally Haslanger, "What is a Social Practice?," *Royal Institute of Philosophy Supplements* 82 (2018), 231–247.

53. See Alexander Sutherland Neill, *The Last Man Alive* (London 1938).

54. For a systematic elaboration of such a view in Durkheim, Hegel, and Marx, see the illuminating study by Fred Neuhouser, *Diagnosing Social Pathologies* (Cambridge 2023).

55. See the reflections of Ann Swidler, who assumes the existence of such "anchor practices." Ann Swidler, "What Anchors Cultural Practices,"

in Theodore Schatzki et al., *The Practice Turn in Contemporary Theory* (New York 2001), 83–101, 90.

56. Jens Beckert, for example, claims that economics has a dominant, orienting function that is specific to our time. See Jens Beckert, "Wirtschaftssoziologie als Gesellschaftstheorie," *Zeitschrift für Soziologie* 38, no. 3 (2009), 182–197. This is not to say that economic practices have exercised the same function in relation to forms of life throughout world history.

57. We should not forget that Marx is formulating an empirical hypothesis here. As Jürgen Habermas has also pointed out, Marx is pursuing a kind of empirically falsifiable philosophy of history. The course of history to date can be understood within this theoretical framework, but the latter needs to be tested against the historical material if it is to be found at all convincing.

58. Karl Marx, trans. David McLellan, "The Poverty of Philosophy," in *Selected Writings* (Oxford: Oxford University Press, 2000), 219; translation modified.

59. Karl Marx, trans. Ben Fowkes, *Capital, A Critique of Political Economy*, Vol. 1 (Harmondsworth: Penguin, 1976), 929.

60. Most of these discussions were prompted by Gerald A. Cohen, *Karl Marx's Theory of History* (Oxford 1978).

61. See Heike Le Ker, "Automaten der Antike: Wie die Götter die Tempeltüren öffneten," *Spiegel Wissenschaft*, 9.4.2009, https://www.spiegel.de/wissenschaft/mensch/automaten-der-antike-wie-die-goetter-dietem peltueren-oeffneten-a-618229.html.

62. This is particularly evident in forms of cooperation. Machine use requires and enables a division of labor, just as the experience of workplace discipline and collaboration shapes subjectivities and changes how people relate to each other. Conversely, the organization of labor has cultural prerequisites: it has its roots in social practices and links to the political form of organization.

63. These considerations also appear in Marxist circles. See Michael Heinrich, *Wissenschaft vom Wert: Die Marxsche Kritik der politischen Ökonomie zwischen wissenschaftlicher Revolution und klassischer Tradition* (Münster 1991). On p. 143 of his book, Heinrich argues with reference to Marx's analyses of art that Marx only emphasizes a "structural dependence," not a mirroring relationship. (There are other

passages in Marx that strike quite a different note, of course.) I owe this reference to Jan van Dick.

64. John Dewey, "Progress," *International Journal of Ethics* 26, no. 3 (1916): 311–322, 313.

65. Barbaric beheadings are posted on the same social media channels where influencers fish for likes and companies advertise their products.

66. See Althusser, "Contradiction and Overdetermination." Social transformation processes, including revolutions at the upper limit, can be overdetermined events in the sense that they are fed by several sources that influence each other. They are the result of different causal chains that at first appear to be unrelated.

4. Crisis and Conflict: The Dynamics of Social Change

Epigraphs: Karl Marx, ed. Joseph O'Malley, "Contribution to the Critique of Hegel's Philosophy of Right," in Marx, *Early Political Writings* (Cambridge, UK: Cambridge University Press, 1994), 65; Thomas Kuhn, *The Structure of Scientific Revolutions: 50th Anniversary Edition* (Chicago: Chicago University Press, 2012), 92; Virginie Despentes, trans. F. Wynne, *Dear Dickhead* (New York: Farrar, Straus & Giroux, 2024).

1. As pointed out in the Introduction, I borrow this concept from Isette Schuhmacher.

2. I here take Marx's reflections on the conditions for revolution to be reflections on radical social change. On how radical social change or accelerated and condensed moments of social transformation relate to revolutions, see Alex Demirović, "Transformation und Ereignis: Zur Dynamik demokratischer Veränderungsprozesse der kapitalistischen Gesellschaftsformation," in Michael Brie, *Futuring: Perspektiven der Transformation im Kapitalismus über ihn hinaus* (Münster: Westfälisches Dampfboot, 2014), 419–435.

3. As the discussion of spousal rape made clear, the question of what "fits" is always one of how the practices at issue are interpreted: whether a particular occurrence is seen as a variant of *sex* (however unpalatable) or *violence* makes all the difference here.

4. On the idea of social changes that take place or gestate in interstitial spaces, see also Michel Foucault's idea of "heterotopias": Foucault, trans. Jay Miskowiec, "Of Other Spaces," *Diacritics* 16, no. 1 (1986), 22–27. For a contemporary application of this model, see Eva von Re-

decker, *Praxis und Revolution: Eine Sozialtheorie radikalen Wandels* (Frankfurt am Main: Campus, 2018). Erik Olin Wright coined the concept of "interstitial transformation," although he also made clear that this cannot be an end in itself. Wright, *Envisioning Real Utopias* (London: Verso, 2010), 435.

5. It is obviously not the case that change always actually occurs when necessary or possible. Dramatic evidence of this can be found in the almost fifty-year history of the industrialized world suppressing or trivializing the ecological threats posed by climate change. Practices that have become obsolete or dysfunctional can sometimes prove remarkably tenacious, as the protracted, hard-fought process of securing rights for women, children, and other discriminated groups shows. But a failure to react only causes the problems to proliferate, and culminates, as we will see in Chapter 6, in regression.

6. The Lenin quote reads: "For a revolution to take place it is not enough for the exploited and oppressed masses to realize the impossibility of living in the old way. It is only when the 'lower classes' do not want to live in the old way and the 'upper classes' cannot carry on in the old way that the revolution can triumph. . . . Revolution is impossible without a nationwide crisis (affecting both the exploiters and the exploited)." Vladimir Lenin, *Learning with Lenin: Selected Works on Education and Revolution,* eds. Derek R. Ford and Curry Malott (Charlotte, NC: Information Age Publishing, 2019), 613. In Thomas Brasch's film *Domino* (Zweites Deutsches Fernsehen, 1982), the message is less encouraging: "The old no longer works and neither does the new."

7. Hannah Arendt, trans. Denver Lindley, "Thoughts on Politics and Revolution," *New York Review of Books*, April 22, 1971: 8-20.

8. For more on "the problem with problems," see Rahel Jaeggi, trans. Ciaran Cronin, *Critique of Forms of Life* (Cambridge, MA: Harvard University Press, 2018), 139–145.

9. G. W. F. Hegel, trans. H. B. Nisbet, *Elements of the Philosophy of Right* (Cambridge, UK: Cambridge University Press, 1991), 199–219.

10. Frederick Neuhouser, *Foundations of Hegel's Social Theory: Actualizing Freedom* (Cambridge, MA: Harvard University Press, 2000), 65.

11. I owe this example to a segment on *Last Week Tonight with John Oliver*, HBO, June 26, 2022, and thank Jan von Dijk for bringing it to my attention.

12. Jürgen Kaube, "Und, schmeckt's?," *Frankfurter Allgemeine Zeitung*, April 27, 2023, 9.

13. See Niklaus Geyrhalter's documentary film *Unser täglich Brot* (Austria 2006)

14. Iris Marion Young, "Throwing Like a Girl: A Phenomenology of Feminine Body Comportment Motility and Spatiality," *Human Studies* 3, no. 1 (1980): 137–156.

15. See Sally Haslanger, "What is a Social Practice?" *Royal Institute of Philosophy Supplements* 82 (2018): 231–247.

16. Bertolt Brecht, trans. J. Willett and R. Manheim, *Poems 1913–1956* (London: Methuen, 1987), 416.

17. Martin Luther King Jr., "Letter from Birmingham Jail," in King, *A Time to Break Silence: The Essential Works of Martin Luther King, Jr., for Students* (Boston: Beacon, 2013), 166–167.

18. G. W. F. Hegel, trans. H. B. Nisbet, *Lectures on the Philosophy of World History* (Cambridge, UK: Cambridge University Press, 1980), 46; translation modified.

19. Karl Marx, *The Eighteenth Brumaire of Louis Napoleon* (New York: International Publishers, 1963), 15.

20. See Elizabeth Anderson, "Social Movements, Experiments in Living, and Moral Progress: Case Studies from Britain's Abolition of Slavery," Lindley Lecture for 2014, University of Kansas, Lawrence, KS, February 11, 2014, 2, text available at https://hdl.handle.net/1808/14787.

21. Leon Trotsky, trans. M. Eastman, *History of the Russian Revolution* (London 2017), ii.

22. See Jaeggi, *Critique of Forms of Life*, 177–189.

23. In fact, freedom of travel had already been decided on at the time, on the assumption that it alone could appease the increasingly powerful protest movement. The only mistake was the abrupt political implementation of the decision, without which events would not have accelerated so massively. Precisely because it happened in so sudden and disorderly a fashion, it reinforced the impression that existing institutions had eroded completely. In retrospect, at least, it sounded the death knell on the old order.

24. See Robert Ziegelmann, *Bestimmende Negation: Utopie und Utopiekritik in Kritischer Theorie,* unpublished dissertation, Humboldt University, Berlin, 2023.

25. Here and in the following sentence, I quote from Robert Frost's "The Road Not Taken," a poem that also gave its name to a December 2022 exhibition at the German Historical Museum in Berlin.

5. Change for the Better? Progress as a Self-Enriching Learning Process

Epigraphs: Kim de l'Horizon, *Blutbuch* (Cologne: DuMont, 2022), 41. A very similar formulation (cited in Chapter 1) appears in Antonio Machado, "CXXXVI Proverbios y cantares," in Machado, trans. Willis Barnstone, *Border of a Dream: Selected Poems of Antonio Machado* (Port Townsend, WA: Copper Canyon, 2013), 281; Helene Hegemann, *Schlachtensee* (Cologne: Kiepenheuer & Witsch, 2022), 183.

1. Robert Musil, trans. Sophie Wilkins, *The Man Without Qualities* (London: Picador, 2017), 528; translation modified. [The German phrase quoted here, "in einem bestimmten Sinn," permits a variety of translations: "in a certain sense" (Wilkins's version), "in a specific meaning," or even "in a particular direction." As we will see, all these meanings work together: if the *sense* of the progress referred to here is "determinate," this is because it moves in a certain *direction* toward a goal that determines its *meaning* as progressive.—Translator's note.]
2. I would like to thank Jakob Huber, in particular, for his incisive critical commentary on this chapter, which helped me clarify some of my claims.
3. Musil, *The Man Without Qualities*, 528; translation modified.
4. The classic study is Wolfgang Schivelbusch, *The Railway Journey: The Industrialization of Time and Space in the Nineteenth Century* (Oakland, CA: University of California Press, 1989).
5. See, for example, the paintings of Eugène Louis Boudin.
6. For a sardonic commentary on such accusations against diversity policy, see Ijoma Mangold, "Alles so schön keimfrei hier," *Die Zeit*, April 24, 2023, https://www.zeit.de/2023/17/kunst-freiheit-moral-ideologie-iden titaetspolitik. This policy is at home in the boardrooms of big corporations and large government institutions. For all that we should be wary of the dangerous alliances that Nancy Fraser has dubbed "progressive neoliberalism," it is no less important to remember the emancipatory roots of these movements, which have long harbored a process of reflection that stands opposed to such affirmatory tendencies.
7. In fact, such benchmarks are commonplace in UN reports and make good pragmatic sense here. On the question of the measurability of quality of life, see Stefan Gosepath, Rahel Jaeggi, and Achim Vesper, "Lebensqualität," in *Handbuch Angewandte Ethik*, eds. Ralf Stoecker et al. (Stuttgart: J. B. Metzler, 2011), 260–264.

8. Karl Marx, trans. Joseph O'Malley, "Contribution to the Critique of Hegel's Philosophy of Right," in Marx, *Early Political Writings* (Cambridge, UK: Cambridge University Press, 1994), 64.

9. If course, it is not only the *ends* of progress that can be controversial but also the *means* for achieving them. Does the washing machine really make housework easier, or does it only lead to higher expectations of spotless laundry? Are antibiotics really a suitable panacea for infections, given their problematic side effects? While these can be difficult questions to answer in individual cases, they do not cast doubt on the overarching goal, the overall *sense of this sense*.

10. See, for example, Amy Allen, who in *The End of Progress: Decolonizing the Normative Foundations of Critical Theory* (New York: Columbia University Press, 2016) assumes the existence of progress at a local level while arguing for the metaethical indeterminacy of progress as such. Philip Kitcher in *The Ethical Project* (Cambridge, MA: Harvard University Press, 2011) likewise characterizes progressive measures as "local" rather than global," although in my view his approach offers resources for the latter.

11. Musil, *The Man Without Qualities*, 528; translation modified.

12. The normativist described in Chapter 1 need not be bothered by this; against ethical relativism, she would insist on a superordinate normative goal. But I expressly argued there that progress, regardless of the metaethical position adopted in relation to the question of relativism, should not be understood as steering toward a preassigned normative goal—another reason why I cannot resort to a simple and substantial universalism.

13. It does not help much to join Amy Allen in describing such a deflationary approach as a "metanormative contextualism," which on her account is compatible with fighting for the norms one embraces (for example, that the end of chattel slavery or female emancipation is good). After all, every plausible relativism already contends that norms are valid relative to a (particular) context, not that they lack all basis for their validity. Precisely if one shares Allen's disinclination, on the one hand, to plunge into the abyss of an "anything goes" relativism while, on the other hand, remaining "open" to the fallibility of one's own epistemological and normative premises, there are in my view still too many open questions here. These could perhaps be better clarified in the tradition of Critical Theory, provided that its social-theoretical

foundations and method of immanent critique were not dismissed *tout court* as Eurocentric. See Allen, *The End of Progress*, 209–219.

14. Ludwig Wittgenstein, trans. G.E.M. Anscombe et al., *Philosophical Investigations* rev. 4th ed. (Chichester: Wiley-Blackwell, 2009), 91.

15. I allude here to Joseph Raz's interpretation of the value of autonomy in western societies in *The Morality of Freedom* (Oxford: Clarendon, 1986), 394.

16. Sigmund Freud, trans. James Strachey, "Civilization and its Discontents," in Freud, *The Standard Edition of the Complete Psychological Works of Sigmund Freud*, Vol. 21 (London: Random House, 2001), 75.

17. Freud, trans. Tania and James Stern, letter to Marie Bonaparte, August 13, 1937, in Freud, *The Letters of Sigmund Freud*, ed. Ernst L. Freud (New York: Dover, 1992), 436; translation modified.

18. See section 1.2 above. Also see Kitcher, *The Ethical Project;* and Kitcher, *Moral Progress* (New York: Oxford University Press, 2021).

19. Musil, *The Man Without Qualities*, 528; translation modified.

20. On witch-burning, see Sylvia Federici, *Caliban and the Witch: Women, the Body and Primitive Accumulation* (London: Penguin, 2021).

21. "From every viewpoint—socially, economically, culturally, politically—the witch-hunt was a turning point in women's lives . . . . For the witch-hunt destroyed a whole world of female practices, collective relations, and systems of knowledge that had been the foundation of women's power in pre-capitalist Europe, and the condition for their resistance in the struggle against feudalism." Federici, *Caliban and the Witch*, 130–131.

22. In a similar vein, Friedrich Engels had warned: "It is very easy to inveigh against slavery and similar things in general terms, and to give vent to high moral indignation at such infamies. . . . But it does not tell us one word as to how these institutions arose, why they existed, and what role they played in history." Friedrich Engels, trans. E. Burns, *Anti-Dühring: Herr Eugen Dühring's Revolution in Science* (Moscow: Foreign Language Publishing House, 1959), 250.

23. See Chapter 3 above, as well as Jaeggi, *Critique of Forms of Life*, ix–xiv and 1–31.

24. To rephrase it in terms of the established debate on forms of critique, doing away with the old meaning stands in this sense for a disconnected and ahistorical external criticism, the analytical-critical stance for immanent critique. See Jaeggi, *Critique of Forms of Life*, Chapter 4

and Rahel Jaeggi, "Was ist Ideologiekritik?" in *Was ist Kritik?*, eds. Rahel Jaeggi and Tilo Wesche (Frankfurt am Main: Suhrkamp, 2009), 266–295.

25. This idea of progress as self-enriching meta-reflection is also suggested by Alasdair MacIntyre's reflections on the rationality of traditions. See my discussion of MacIntyre in *Critique of Forms of Life*, 221–236.

26. See Daniel Loick, *Die Überlegenheit der Unterlegenen: Eine Theorie der Gegengemeinschaften* (Berlin: Suhrkamp, 2024).

27. For a highly instructive attempt to elaborate such a concept of experience with explicit reference to Dewey, see Tanja Bogusz, *Experimentalismus und Soziologie: Von der Krisen- zur Erfahrungswissenschaft* (Frankfurt am Main: Campus, 2018), 59–75.

28. The motif appears in his reflections on the loss of the capacity to experience. See Walter Benjamin, trans. R. Livingstone, "The Storyteller," in Benjamin, *Selected Writings: Volume 3, 1935–1938* (Cambridge, MA: Harvard University Press, 2006), 143–166, and Benjamin, trans. R. Livingstone, "Experience and Poverty," in *Selected Writings: Volume 2, Part 2, 1931–1934* (Cambridge, MA: Harvard University Press, 2005), 731–736.

29. John Dewey, "Progress," *International Journal of Ethics* 26, no. 3 (1916): 311–322.

30. Naturally, there are differences here within the pragmatist camp. Hilary Putnam takes Dewey to mean that progress can be evaluated without limiting it to local validity, and this without any need for a metaphysical basis or ultimate justification: "Dewey believes (as we all do, when we are not playing the skeptic) that there are better and worse resolutions to human predicaments—to what he calls 'problematic situations.'" Hilary Putnam, "A Reconsideration of Deweyan Democracy," in *The Pragmatism Reader: From Peirce through the Present*, eds. Robert B. Talisse and Scott F. Aikin (Princeton: Princeton University Press, 2011), 338. By contrast, Richard Rorty's interpretation of Dewey points in exactly the opposite direction. For Rorty, a pragmatically oriented assessment of cultural differences and historical development must restrict itself to a local and contingent narrative. See Richard Rorty, "Rationality and Cultural Difference," in *Truth and Progress: Philosophical Papers* (Cambridge, UK: Cambridge University Press, 1991), 186–201.

31. By "lacunae," I allude here to the concept of the "hermeneutical lacuna" developed by Miranda Fricker in *Epistemic Injustice: Power*

and the Ethics of Knowing (Oxford: Oxford University Press, 2007), 150–161.

32. Theodor W. Adorno, trans. Henry W. Pickford, "Progress," in *Critical Models: Interventions and Catchwords* (New York: Columbia University Press, 2005), 143–160, 160.

33. Adorno, "Progress," 144.

34. I borrow the idea of a "rational responding" from Robert Ziegelmann, *Bestimmende Negation: Utopie und Utopiekritik in Kritischer Theorie* unpublished dissertation, Humboldt University, Berlin 2023.

35. Friedrich Engels, *The Condition of the Working Class in England* [1845] (Oxford 2009).

36. Upton Sinclair, *The Jungle* (New York: Doubleday, 1906).

37. See Mel Gussow, "Theater: Improvisation On Sinclair's 'Jungle,'" *New York Times*, December 10, 1983, http://www.nytimes.com/1983/12/10 /theater/theater-improvisation-on-sinclair-s-jungle.html. Sinclair evidently read *Uncle Tom's Cabin* as an abolitionist novel, ignoring the much-criticized aspects of the novel that concern the passive role of those depicted.

38. Karl Marx, "The Duchess of Sutherland and Slavery," *The People's Paper* 45, March 12, 1853.

39. "This worker must be free in the double sense that as a free individual he can dispose of his labor-power as his own commodity, and that, on the other hand, he has no other commodity for sale, i.e. he is rid of them, he is free of all the objects needed for the realization . . . of his labor-power." Karl Marx, trans. Ben Fowkes, *Capital: A Critique of Political Economy: Volume 1* (London: Penguin, 1990), 272–273.

40. The experience of "black reconstruction" shows that political emancipation alone does not suffice and that conditions of slavery can in some respects be recreated under the guise of wage labor. See W. E. B. Du Bois, *Black Reconstruction in America: 1860–1880* (New York: Russell & Russell, 1935).

41. See Karl Marx, trans. David Fernbach, *Capital: A Critique of Political Economy: Volume 3* (London: Penguin, 1992), Chapter 47.

42. Marx, *Capital: Volume 1*, 486.

43. Marx, *Capital: Volume 3*, 958.

44. See Sven Beckert, *Empire of Cotton: A Global History* (New York: Knopf, 2014), and Andreas Eckert, "Keine Moderne ohne verschleppte Sklaven," *Frankfurter Allgemeine Zeitung*, April 6, 2023, https://www .faz.net/aktuell/feuilleton/buecher/rezensionen/sachbuch/afrika

-und-derwesten-keine-moderne-ohne-verschleppte-sklaven-18788483
.html.

45. This goes some way to addressing the suspicion, mentioned at the outset, that concepts of progress make it hard to see and thematize forms of domination that persist in reality after a certain form has been superseded, such as the de facto continuation of slavery and unfree labor in modern slavery or in the US prison system. This may well be a danger for optimistic liberal theories of progress. From the perspective of a critical theory, as indicated here with recourse to Marx, it should be possible to understand what is specific to old slavery and what is new in modern slavery. This is not so much a normative question, a question of whether one form of slavery is worse than the other. And the perspective I am adopting explicitly avoids understanding modern slavery as a remnant or mere deviation from the "liberal script." Rather, it is the particular possibilities for overcoming them that differ from each other, depending on the historical and social context in which the relevant practices are situated. From a liberal perspective, it may seem puzzling that exploitation resembling slavery still exists under conditions of political and legal freedom. Modern slavery here appears as normatively highly problematic yet ultimately anachronistic. My position, by contrast, seeks to analyze the various functions and modes of operation of old and new slavery in order to work toward their overcoming. I thank Robin Celikates for discussions on this point.

46. See, for example, Gisela Bock, trans. A. Brown, *Women in European History* (London: Wiley, 2002), and Karin Hausen, *Geschlechtergeschichte als Gesellschaftsgeschichte* (Göttingen: Vandenhoeck & Ruprecht, 2013).

47. Undine Eberlein, *Einzigartigkeit: Das romantische Individualitätskonzept der Moderne* (Frankfurt am Main: Campus, 2000), 352.

48. On dualist versus deficitary interpretations, see also Thomas Laqueur, *Making Sex. Bodies and Gender from the Greeks to Freud* (Cambridge, MA: Harvard University Press, 1990). On the process by which the sexual difference was displaced onto nature, see Claudia Honegger, *Die Ordnung der Geschlechter: Die Wissenschaft vom Menschen und das Weib, 1750–1850* (Frankfurt am Main: Suhrkamp, 1991).

49. I borrow here the title of Charlotte Wood's visionary feminist fable, *The Natural Way of Things* (Sydney: Allen & Unwin, 2015).

50. Eberlein, *Einzigartigkeit*, 352.
51. Gisela Bock and Barbara Duden, "Labor of Love—Love as Labor: On the Genesis of Housework in Capitalism," in *From Feminism to Liberation*, ed. Edith Hoshino Altback (Cambridge, MA: Schenkman, 1980), 153–192.
52. "Shadow work" is the term given in some feminist discourses to the fact that in our society, women's (house)work is often overshadowed by wage labor, which has primarily masculine connotations. Shadow work is unpaid, publicly unrecognized, and precarious. It also widely seen as merely a factor in the reproduction of male labor, without any status and social security of its own. Ivan Illich coined the term, which was subsequently taken up and reinterpreted in feminist discussion. See Ivan Illich, "Shadow-Work," *Philosophica* 26 (1980): 7–46.
53. Eberlein, *Einzigartigkeit*, 352.
54. Eric J. Hobsbawm, *The Age of Revolution, 1789–1848* (London: Abacus, 1988), 2.
55. Why the new economic order relied on the idea of equality and, conversely, why the idea of equality lent it plausibility, is another story. It has been told by Marx (in one direction) and Sewell (in another).

6. Betrayal of the Possible: On the Anatomy of Regression

Epigraphs: Theodor W. Adorno, trans. Robert Hullot-Kentor, *Philosophy of New Music* (Minneapolis: University of Minnesota Press, 2006), 10; Georg Diez, "Ablenkungsmanöver. Wenn Gedichte zu 'Fake News' werden," *Spiegel Online*, February 4, 2018, http://www.spiegel .de/kultur/gesellschaft/ablenkungsmanoever-wenn-gedichte-zu-fake -news-werden-kolumne-a-1190973.html.
1. As noted in the Preface, the frequency with which "regression" is diagnosed today is remarkable not least from a methodological standpoint. The use of a term so closely associated with psychoanalysis (albeit not monopolized by it) suggests a blending of social analysis with questions of social psychology reminiscent of the first generation of the Frankfurt School. This aspect of Critical Theory has not exactly taken center stage in recent decades, although it has been attracting more attention of late. It is in keeping with this upswing in interest that the concept of the "authoritarian personality" and studies on the authori-

tarian character appear to be undergoing a minor renaissance. Peter Gordon paved the way in "The Authoritarian Personality Revisited: Reading Adorno in the Age of Trump," *b2o: An Online Journal*, June 15, 2016, https://www.boundary2.org/2016/06/peter-gordon-the-au thoritarian-personality-revisited-reading-adorno-in-the-age-of-trump/.

2. R. Jay Wallace attributes a comparable contrast between a high-profile public life, on the one hand, and a weakly contoured philosophical life, on the other, to the concept of ressentiment. See Wallace, "Ressenti- ment, Value, and Self-Vindication: Making Sense of Nietzsche's Slave Revolt," in *Nietzsche and Morality*, eds. Brian Leiter and Neil Sinha- babu (Oxford: Oxford University Press, 2007), 110–137.

3. Svenja Ahlhaus and Peter Niesen contend that that the diagnosis of regression often articulates nothing more than a vague holistic impres- sion, a generalized understanding of social pathologies. See Svenja Ahl- haus and Peter Niesen, "Regressionen des Mitgliedschaftsrechts: Für einen Kosmopolitismus von innen," in *Kritische Theorie der Politik*, eds. Paul Sörensen and Ulf Bohmann (Berlin: Suhrkamp, 2019), 608–631.

4. Jürgen Körner, "Regression—Progression," in *Handbuch psychoanaly- tischer Grundbegriffe*, eds. Wolfgang Mertens and Bruno Waldvogel (Stuttgart: Kohlhammer, 2008), 633–639.

5. See Sigmund Freud, trans. J. Strachey, "Remembering, Repeating, and Working-through," in *The Standard Edition of the Complete Psycho- logical Works of Sigmund Freud*, ed. J. Strachey, Vol. 12 (London: Random House, 2001), 145–156.

6. See Ernst Kris, "Zur Psychologie der Karikatur," *Imago* 20, no. 4 (1934): 450–466, 454.

7. See Michael Bálint, *The Basic Fault: Therapeutic Aspects of Regression* (Evanston, IL: Northwestern University Press, 1992), 147. Hans Loewald describes the therapeutic use of regression in a similar way: "Analysis is thus understood as an intervention designed to set ego- development in motion, be it from a point of relative arrest, or to pro- mote what we conceive of as a healthier direction and/or comprehen- siveness of such development. This is achieved by the promotion and utilization of (controlled) regression." Hans Loewald, *Papers on Psy- choanalysis* (New Haven: Yale University Press, 1980), 224. I thank Marvin Ester for directing me to these references.

8. Michael Bálint vividly describes the funfair in these terms: "The tradi- tional foods sold at funfairs must generally have two characteristics—

they must be very sweet and very cheap. Often the type of sweets sold there are peculiar to funfairs and are sold hardly anywhere else or on any other occasions; this, however, is not an absolute rule. The next group comprises the aggressive games, such as target shooting, tests of strength, and even purely destructive ones like 'breaking up the happy home,' where cheap china is displayed to be smashed up with wooden balls. The psychodynamics of these two groups of pleasures can be described up to a point by our existing terminology. They both represent opportunities for regression, i.e., they offer satisfaction for primitive instincts on a fairly primitive level: the first group to the oral, and the second to the destructive or aggressive instincts. Seen from this angle, funfairs are safety valves for pent-up emotions and instinctual urges which, in civilized and well-brought-up adults, must remain unsatisfied, and which are offered periodic outlets on a primitive level within safe limits." Michael Bálint, *Thrills and Regressions* (Abingdon, UK: Routledge, 2018), 23.

9. Adorno, *Philosophy of New Music*, trans. Robert Hullot-Kentor (Minneapolis: University of Minnesota Press, 2019), 10.

10. Of course, returning to the multigenerational principle will only prove effective where it is combined with modern teaching materials and state-of-the-art pedagogic principles and techniques.

11. The founder of the company, which uses "the good old things" as an advertising slogan, is known for his ties with institutions on the far right. Thomas Hoof, Manufactuam's owner until 2008, heads the far-right publishing house Manuscriptum; its stable of authors includes Björn Höcke, Frank Böckelmann, and Akif Pirinçci. See, for example, "Akif Pirinçci: Manufactum distanziert sich wegen Pirinçci-Buch von Firmengründer," *Zeit Online*, April 8, 2014, https://www.zeit.de /kultur/literatur/2014–04/manufactum-akif-pirincci-verlag-manu scriptum-distanzierung.

12. On the genre of the *Heimatfilm*: "The 1950s in West Germany: towns still bear the scars of war, families are shattered, and a new film genre becomes a homegrown success story: *Heimatfilme* draw thousands into the cinemas. In the years after 1945, hardly anyone in Germany felt at home in their immediate surroundings. Amid the countless dead, the bombed-out cities, and the feelings of guilt, there arose a deep longing for a still intact world, a cozy *Heimat*. The *Heimatfilm* offered just that. And for a couple of hours, at least, viewers could immerse themselves in this cinematic world." Ulrike Vosberg, "Der Deutsche

Heimatfilm," *Planet Wissen* website, 2016. The perennial Christmas favorite, *Die Feuerzangenbowle* (shot in 1944!), and the postwar popularity of actor Heinz Rühmann provide other good examples: presenting the Second German Empire as a lovable oddity rather than as an authoritarian prelude to fascism is already a questionable move. Helmut Weiss, dir., *Die Feuerzangenbowle,* Ufa Studios, Potsdam-Babelsberg, 1944. On Rühmann, see this excellent essay: Helma Sanders-Brahms, "Ein kleiner Mann," in *Das Dunkle zwischen den Bildern: Essays, Porträts, Kritiken,* ed. Norbert Grob (Frankfurt am Main: Autoren, 1992), 68–77.

13. Hannah Arendt, *Besuch in Deutschland* (Berlin: Rotbuch, 1993), 24. It is sometimes difficult to draw a line between nostalgia and regression. For example, there is ongoing controversy over whether the rebuilding of the Berlin Palace is a harmless reconstruction of the nineteenth-century cityscape, a dangerous expression of reactionary tendencies that seeks to brush over the changes to the city caused by National Socialism and the Second World War, or merely a symptom of the exhaustion of modernism in urban architecture and design.

14. Another recent example is the ruling on abortion made by the US Supreme Court.

15. On the concept of restoration, see Carl Ludwig von Haller, *Restauration der Staats-Wissenschaft oder Theorie des natürlich-geselligen Zustands, der Chimäre des künstlich-bürgerlichen entgegengesetzt* (Aalen: Scientia, 1964), reprint of the 2nd edition (Winterthur: Steinerischen, 1834).

16. See Oliver Nachtwey, trans. David Fernbach and Loren Balhorn, *Germany's Hidden Crisis: Social Decline in the Heart of Europe* (London: Verso, 2018).

17. On the theory and critique of the welfare state, see Stephan Lessenich, *Theorien des Sozialstaats zur Einführung* (Hamburg: Junius, 2012).

18. I can do no more than sketch this argument here to illustrate the structural aspects of regression. See the illuminating intervention from Emma Dowling and Silke van Dyk, "Rückkehr des Hauptwiderspruchs? Anmerkungen zur aktuellen Debatte um den Erfolg der Neuen Rechten und das Versagen der 'Identitätspolitik,'" *PROKLA* 47, no. 3 (2007), 411–420.

19. Walter Benjamin, trans. H. Zohn, "Theses on the Philosophy of History," in Benjamin, *Illuminations* (London: Pimlico, 1999), 245–255, 257 (Thesis VIII).

20. Adorno and Horkheimer describe their book's intention as seeking to understand "why humanity, instead of entering a truly human state, is sinking into a new kind of barbarism." Max Horkheimer and Theodor W. Adorno, trans. E. Jephcott, *Dialectic of Enlightenment* (Stanford: Stanford University Press, 2002), xiv.

21. Theodor W. Adorno, "Freudian Theory and the Pattern of Fascist Propaganda," in *The Essential Frankfurt School Reader,* eds. Andrew Arato and Eike Gebhardt (New York: Urizen, 1978), 118–137, 122.

22. Horkheimer and Adorno, *Dialectic of Enlightenment,* xiv.

23. See Claus Offe, trans. R. Libermann and J. Wengrofsky, "Modern 'Barbarity': A Micro-State of Nature," *Constellations* 2, no. 3 (1996): 355–377.

24. Theodor W. Adorno, trans. R. Livingstone, *History and Freedom: Lectures 1964–1965* (Cambridge, UK: Polity, 2006), 105.

25. That is to say: those who constitute a nation are turned into members of a nation through their communal socialization in relation to a common language, literature, customs, traditions, etc. See Benedict Anderson, *Imagined Communities: Reflections on the Origin and Spread of Nationalism* (New York: Verso, 1983).

26. This is still emancipatory, in principle, because it establishes the people as sovereign over the nobility, even if it is accompanied by problematic inclusions and exclusions. To forestall one obvious objection at this point: Adorno is speaking here of a particular line of development in European history. This does not necessarily imply that world history is steering a normative course toward statehood and the nation-state (as its current, possibly transient manifestation).

27. Adorno, *History and Freedom,* 107.

28. Adorno, *History and Freedom,* 111. Adorno shares this insight with Helmuth Plessner; see Plessner, *Die verspätete Nation: Über die politische Verführbarkeit bürgerlichen Geistes* (Frankfurt am Main: Suhrkamp, 1994).

29. Adorno argues elsewhere, too, that nationalism has lost its basis in reality: "The characteristic form of absurd opinion today is nationalism. With new virulence it infects the entire world, in a historical period where, because of the state of the technical forces of production and the potential definition of the earth as a single planet, at least in the non-underdeveloped countries nationalism has lost its real basis and has become the full-blown ideology it always has been." Theodor W. Adorno, trans. H. Pickford, "Opinion Delusion Society," in *Critical*

Models: Interventions and Catchwords (New York: Columbia University Press, 2005), 105–121, 117–118.

30. The dynamic described here may equally be applied to the contemporary reality of migrant (or postmigrant) societies, global refugee movements, and the populist backlash to them. If Adorno refers to cosmopolitanism as it had developed in his own day, based on the real interdependence of living conditions, then today's dispiriting spectacle of walls, borders, tub-thumping xenophobic nationalism, and the playing off of so-called cosmopolitan elites against parochial loyalties is inappropriate in a very similar way to that meant by Adorno.

31. Adorno, *History and Freedom*, 110; translation modified.

32. Adorno, *History and Freedom*, 110.

33. Sabine Hark, *Gemeinschaft der Ungewählten: Umrisse eines politischen Ethos der Kohabitation* (Berlin: Suhrkamp, 2021).

34. See David Goodhart, *The Road to Somewhere: The Populist Revolt and the Future of Politics* (London: Hurst, 2017).

35. For a qualitative study of Trump voters in the United States that confirms this observation, see Arlie Russell Hochschild, *Strangers in Their Own Land: Anger and Mourning on the American Right* (New York: New Press, 2016).

36. Interestingly, the mobilization against so-called gender ideology is worldwide; it extends from the AfD in Germany through US state governors and Brazilian evangelicals to propaganda in Putin's Russia that equates Westernization with decadence and emasculation. See, for example, Niklas Franzen, "Bolsonaros deutsche Freundin," taz.de, December 2, 2022, https://taz.de/AfDAbgeordnete-und-Brasiliens-Rechte/!5895617/.

37. For a more detailed analysis of ressentiment as a case of regression, see Rahel Jaeggi, "Modes of Regression: The Case of Ressentiment," *Critical Times* 1 (2023): 501–537.

38. The phrase is borrowed from a book first published in 1941: Erich Fromm's *The Fear of Freedom* (London: Routledge, 2001). On debates around gender and the family, see the contributions in Sabine Hark and Paula-Irene Villa, eds., *Anti-Genderismus: Sexualität und Geschlecht als Schauplätze aktueller politischer Auseinandersetzungen* (Bielefeld: Transcript, 2015).

39. See Körner, "Regression—Progression."

40. Habermas was strongly criticized for understanding the psychoanalytic cure in just this way; see Jürgen Habermas, trans. Jeremy J. Sha-

piro, *Knowledge and Human Interests* (Cambridge: Polity, 2015), Chapter 10.

41. "But these two discoveries—that the life of our sexual instincts cannot be wholly tamed, and that mental processes are in themselves unconscious and only reach the ego and come under its control through incomplete and untrustworthy perceptions—these two discoveries amount to a statement that *the ego is not master in its own house.*" Sigmund Freud, trans. J. Strachey, "A Difficulty in the Path of Psychoanalysis," in *The Standard Edition of the Complete Psychological Works of Sigmund Freud,* ed. J. Strachey, Vol. 17 (London: Random House, 2001), 143.

42. Like Hegel before him, and in line with recent discussions on "relational autonomy," Freud conceives autonomy as something that arises not through disregarding other people and their concerns, but by referring meaningfully to them.

43. For more on such inaccessibility, see the reconstruction of the alienation motif proposed in Rahel Jaeggi, trans. F. Neuhouser and A. Smith, *Alienation* (New York: Columbia University Press, 2014), Chapter 5.

44. On the reactive character of contemporary misogyny, see Kate Manne, *Down Girl: The Logic of Misogyny* (New York: Oxford University Press, 2017).

45. On the question of the relationship between the critique of power and the approach I developed in *Critique of Forms of Life*, based on social problem-solving and experiential processes, see my reply to Martin Saar's criticism in Rahel Jaeggi, "Macht, Problem, Kritik: Repliken auf Saar, Crary, Menke und Khurana," in *Philosophisches Jahrbuch* 126 (2019): 321–350.

46. In keeping with this finding, it is possible to argue with political conservatives about the need for change, its extent and speed, but not with regressive reactionaries. See also Mathias Greffrath, "Das Herz schlägt rechts: Wo bleiben die wahren Konservativen? Die mit intellektuellem Anspruch Pläne für eine lebenswerte Zukunft entwickeln?," *taz online,* February 23, 2020, https://taz.de/Konservative-Heimatsehnsuechte /!5661469/.

47. See John Dewey, *Democracy and Education: An Introduction to the Philosophy of Education*, ed. Jo Ann Boydston (Carbondale, IL: Southern Illinois University Press, 1980), 50: "In learning an action, instead of having it given readymade, one of necessity learns to vary its

factors, to make varied combinations of them, according to change of circumstances. A possibility of continuing progress is opened up by the fact that in learning one act, methods are developed good for use in other situations. Still more important is the fact that the human being acquires a habit of learning. He learns to learn."

48. Armin Schäfer and Michael Zürn, *Die demokratische Regression: Die politischen Ursachen des autoritären Populismus* (Berlin: Suhrkamp, 2021).

49. See Jürgen Habermas, trans. Thomas McCarthy, *Legitimation Crisis* (Boston: Beacon, 1975), 15.

50. Karl Marx and Friedrich Engels, *The Communist Manifesto* (London: Verso, 2012), 40.

51. Theodor W. Adorno, trans. A. Rabinbach, "On the Fetish-Character in Music and the Regression of Listening," in Adorno, *Essays on Music,* ed. Richard Leppert (Berkeley: University of California Press, 2002): 288–317, 311. Both here and in the quotation that provides this chapter's with its epigraph, we see how strongly Adorno remained committed in a negative way to a philosophical model of history as a process of development or enrichment, despite criticizing it explicitly. See Isette Schuhmacher, "Fortschritt nach Adorno," unpublished Master's thesis, Humboldt University, Berlin, 2017. See now also Rahel Jaeggi and Isette Schuhmacher, "Adorno's Negative Philosophy of History," in *Oxford Handbook to Adorno,* eds. Martin Shuster and Henry Pickford (forthcoming from Oxford University Press).

52. See Rosa Luxemburg, "The Junius Pamphlet: The Crisis in German Social Democracy," in *The Rosa Luxemburg Reader,* eds. Peter Hudis and Kevin B. Anderson (New York: Monthly Review, 2004), 312–379, 350. We now know how alarmingly prescient Rosa Luxemburg's prognosis was. A similar pattern of regression is described in Karl Polanyi's theory of how society reacts to the absolutization of the market, which disembedded economic activities from social practices and orientations. If society defends itself against the destructive marketization and disembedding of the economy, it can do so in either a fascist-regressive or a progressive-socialist direction. See Karl Polanyi, *The Great Transformation: The Political and Economic Origins of Our Time* (Boston: Beacon Press, 2001).

ACKNOWLEDGMENTS

This book took far longer to complete than originally planned—partly due to external factors, partly for reasons intrinsic to the subject matter. Some of it was simply bad luck and couldn't be avoided. I wish to thank everyone who, despite all the hurdles in my path, helped me across the finish line.

I could always count on Fred Neuhouser and Eugene O'Keefe for their support. Without my walks with Anna Riek, Regina Kreide, Tilo Wesche, Petra Eggers, and Christoph Menke, as well as outings and trips with Sabine Hark and Ilona Pache, life during (and after) the pandemic would have been so much harder. I remained in constant contact with Robin Celikates and Martin Saar on important questions concerning life and philosophy. I was also sustained by my friendship and philosophical-political exchanges with Nancy Fraser and Eli Zaretzky.

Isette Schuhmacher, Eva von Redecker, and Lukas Kübler were willing to discuss ideas with me from the moment the book was conceived. Later, Christian Schmidt shared his views on a project he regarded with deep suspicion, watched over its progress, and transformed it through his helpful suggestions. Alex Demirović's insatiable appetite for intellectual debate has always inspired me. Robin Celikates's and Martin Saar's skepticism toward the concept of progress has sharpened the project, as have conversations with Amy Hallen. Thomas Seibert's pugnacity strengthened my resolve, as did discussions with Yves Winter. This book—and much else besides—could not have been written without critical encouragement from Axel Honneth and Fred Neuhouser. In their own ways, Terry Pinkard, Philip Kitcher, Henry Richardson, and Alice Crary stood philosophical godparents to this project; the book owes a great deal to their philosophical work and tireless intellectual companionship. Without Isette Schuhmacher, I would never have understood Adorno's ambivalence toward the philosophy of history. She knows this project better than anyone else—myself included. Robert Ziegelmann spurred me on with his trenchant observations. Finally, Marvin Ester, Carina Nagel, Louis Leary, Josefine Berkholz, Gelareh Shapneh, and Friedemann Melcher were indispensable proofreaders, tracked down hard-to-find references with forensic determination, and improved the book with illuminating quotations. The final chapters benefited additionally from Marvin Ester's extensive knowledge of psychoanalysis. Eva Gilmer wrestled with this book beyond the limits of human endurance. Even more than for her peerless editing and tireless support of a manuscript that seemed at times to have ground to a halt, I thank her for her understanding and friendship.

This book has been fertilized by discussions facilitated by a range of people and institutions. At different stages, I was fortunate enough to present my ideas at colloquia and events at Columbia University, the New School for Social Research, Harvard University, the University of Chicago, Georgetown University, Penn State University, the Institute for Advanced Study, the Center for Human Value in Princeton, and the University of California, Berkeley. I also had the opportunity to give them test runs in Magdeburg, Marburg, Hamburg, Frankfurt am Main, Munich, Turin, and Rome.

Seminars at Humboldt University and the New School for Social Research allowed me to develop my ideas in conversation with students. The Theodor Heuss Professorship at the New School provided me with a stimulating year abroad, while a grant from the German Research Foundation made it possible for me to explore my ideas in greater depth in the form of a summer school and a conference involving some of the key figures in the field.

The final impetus for publication came from a manuscript workshop initiated by Jakob Huber and his research group, "Democratic Hope," held at our Berlin Center for Social Critique. I wish to thank Jakob Huber, in particular, but also his co-organizers—Christian Schmidt, Zveta Paul, and Robin Celikates—for encouraging me to take the plunge. My special thanks go to the commentators who took the trouble to engage with my ideas: Kristina Lepold, Anna Katarina Sodoma, Peter Dews, Maeve Cooke, Dirk Quadflieg, Hauke Brunkhorst, and Robin Celikates; but I am grateful to everyone else who contributed to an unexpectedly gratifying, intensive, and engaged discussion. Further written and verbal comments on the manuscript from Titus Stahl, Daniel Loick, Fred Neuhouser, Regina Kreide, Tilo Wesche, Stefan Gosepath, and Bastian Ronge did much to smooth its progress. Being able to bounce ideas off so many colleagues and friends in an atmosphere of mutual trust is an immense privilege. Albrecht Wellmer used to say that Critical Theory is not a "school" but an ongoing dialogue. His observation has been marvelously confirmed.

Last but not least, the English version could not have appeared so quickly and unproblematically were it not for the exemplary professionalism of my translator, Robert Savage, who produced a translation that was both elegant and accurate in a very short space of time, and the resolution of my editor, Joseph Pomp, who offered to publish the book even before I had finished writing it. I am grateful to them both.

INDEX

accumulation of progress, 3, 5, 9
Adorno, Theodor W., 1, 8, 30,
184n22; on cosmopolitanism,
210n30; *Dialectic of Enlightenment* (with Horkheimer),
157–158, 209n20; on nationalism, 209n29; on philosophy of
history, 8–9, 12; on progress, 1,
20, 21, 137; on regression, 148,
149, 152, 154–155, 157–161,
171, 212n51; on unreduced
experience, 33
alienation, 24, 136, 158
Althusser, Louis, 84
Anderson, Benedict, 159
Anderson, Elizabeth, 52, 55, 59,
70–71
Appiah, Kwame Anthony, 65
Arendt, Hannah, 93, 154
articulation model, 44
authoritarianism: increase in, 174n8;
The Last Man Alive and, 77;
neo-authoritarianism, 10;

paternalism and, 166–167; refugee
crises and, 102; regression and, 25,
157, 161–162, 166, 174n11;
regressive rebel character and,
174n11; Second German Empire
and, 208n12
authoritarian personality,
205–206n1
autonomy, 24, 41, 42, 78, 96, 125,
150, 151, 165, 166

Bálint, Michael, 150, 206–207n8
Bateson, Gregory, 142
Benjamin, Walter, 6, 7, 11, 133, 157
Bhambra, Gurminder K., 12, 180n37
Bock, Gisela, 143
Brecht, Bertolt, 108

capitalism, 42, 83, 86, 87–88, 105;
qualitative expansion of possibilities and, 139–141; regression and,
139–141, 143, 158, 159; slavery
and, 139–141